D1572889

CREATIVE SEWING

CREATIVE SEWING

BY THE EDITORS OF
LADIES' HOME JOURNAL NEEDLE&CRAFT

 MASON/CHARTER   NEW YORK 1977

Copyright © Downe Communications, Inc. 1977

All Rights Reserved

No part of this book may be reproduced in any form
without permission in writing from the publisher

1 2 3 4 5 6 7 8 9 10

Library of Congress Cataloging in Publication Data

Main entry under title:

Creative sewing.

   1. Sewing. I. Ladies' home journal needle &
craft.
TT705.C77 1977   646.2   77–22771
ISBN 0–88405–478–0
ISBN 0–88405–479–9 pbk.

CONTENTS

INTRODUCTION

Sewing is such a sensuous pleasure. Fabric is the lure —you can see its lush colors and its splendid patterns, feel its soft textures and know that here is beauty you can possess. Fabric exists complete in itself, a delight to the eye and hand and heart. And yet it awaits, a medium for your imagination. You can take the quiet cloth and transform it into something three-dimensional and marvelous, your own vision of what it was meant to become. (And it's such a comforting thing to do, relaxing into the rhythm of the sewing machine as it stitches, watching what you have contemplated steadily take shape.) It's a satisfying way of expressing yourself, of getting exactly what you would like to have to reflect your own uniqueness.

Let your love of fabric lead you where it will. Learn to work without patterns, or to graph your own, or to use a classic pattern as a point of departure. Use traditional materials in innovative ways and unexpected materials in simple designs. Create your own patchwork fabric, tie-dye your own fabric, add texture to your fabric with trapunto stitching. Personalize and embellish your designs with appliqué, stencil or embroidery. Once you discover the possibilities and learn the techniques, your sense of style will touch everything you sew.

You'll find that to transform skill into art with exuberance is the essence of creativity.

—Joyce Denebrink
Editor, Mason/Charter

BASIC SEWING

You can create all our designs with your own knowledge of sewing and our simple directions.

For some of the designs you need no patterns at all, just the instructions you will find on how to cut the fabric.

For other designs, you just follow the diagrams that show you how to lay out and cut the pieces directly on the fabric.

Sometimes you will make your own patterns by enlarging the patterns on the graphs. It's easy: just see the chart below, HOW TO ENLARGE AND REDUCE DESIGNS.

Occasionally you will use one of your own classic patterns, one that you know will fit you exactly and is similar to the style in the photograph. If you decide to buy a new pattern and want to determine what size is closest to your own, follow the instructions on HOW TO TAKE BODY MEASUREMENTS. Then compare your own measurements with the "standard body measurements" used by pattern companies and buy the pattern size indicated.

If you have a favorite piece of fabric that you'd like to use and it's not the same width as that called for in the directions, you can look at HOW TO ESTIMATE YARDAGE to find out if the amount you have is the amount you need.

HOW TO ENLARGE AND REDUCE DESIGNS

When enlarging or reducing designs, it is important that the design stay in proportion. Either of these two methods can be used:

METHOD 1
Make a tracing of the design if it is not already marked off in squares. Depending on the size, now mark off with squares. Use ⅛" squares for small designs, ¼", ½", 1" squares etc. for larger designs. After you have decided on the size of the enlargement or reduction, mark off on tracing paper the same number of squares, similarly placed, in the area to be occupied by the design. For example, if you wish to make your design four times as large, make each square four times as large. Now copy the outline from your tracing onto the new squares, square by square.

METHOD 2
Make a tracing of the original design. Put an outline around the tracing. Now, as in the diagram, draw a second outline of the final size (this outline will be below and next to the first, corners touching). The new outline is made by drawing a diagonal line through the

original, continuing it down through one corner as shown, thus being able to perfectly proportion the new size. Now draw the second diagonal line through both outlines. At the point where the two diagonal lines meet at the center draw one horizontal and one vertical line (you now have four equal areas in each outline). In each of these, complete the other diagonals and then divide further into equal rectangles with additional horizontal and vertical lines. As in Method 1, copy the design from the original, tracing it onto the new outline, triangle by triangle. To transfer design onto material to be decorated slip dressmaker's carbon between tracing and surface. Trace carefully with sharp pencil.

An easy way to divide the rectangle into the spaces described above is to fold a paper the desired size of the design into halves, quarters, sixteenths, etc. Other shortcuts: (1) place a wire screen over the original design for squaring-off; (2) transfer the original design to graph paper . . . clear acetate if available.

METHOD 1

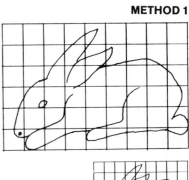

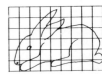

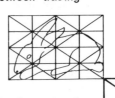

METHOD 2

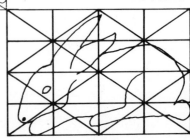

HOW TO TAKE BODY MEASUREMENTS: To determine correct size for patterns for your garments, take body measurements as directed. For misses', women's, juniors' and teens' sizes (while wearing usual under garments), measure at the fullest part of the bust and hips and at the natural waistline. Allowances have been made for ease to insure a proper fit. Any adjustments in size differential between the measurements can be made during the sewing and finishing. Men's and children's sizes are both determined by the size of the chest, the tape being held comfortably over the fullest part of the chest. (**NOTE:** children's sizes are determined by chest measurements, not age. Use other measurements for adjustments while garment is being made.)

STANDARD BODY MEASUREMENTS

All measurements in inches.

JUNIORS

Size	7	9	11	13	15
Bust	31	32	33½	35	37
Waist	22½	23½	24½	26	28
Hip	33	34	35½	37	39

TEENS

Size	7/8	9/10	11/12	13/14
Bust	29	30½	32	33½
Waist	23	24	25	26
Hip	32	33½	35	36½

MISSES

Size	8	10	12	14	16	18
Bust	31½	32½	34	36	38	40
Waist	23	24	25½	27	29	31
Hip	33½	34½	36	38	40	42

WOMEN

Size	38	40	42	44	46	48
Bust	42	44	46	48	50	52
Waist	34	36	38	40½	43	45½
Hip	44	46	48	50	52	54

MEN

Size	34	36	38	40	42	44
Chest	34	36	38	40	42	44
Waist	30	32	34	36	38	40

INFANTS AND GIRLS

Size	6 mos.	1	2	3	4	6	8	10	12	14
Chest	19	20	21	22	23	24	27	28½	30	32
Waist	19	19½	20	20½	21	22	23½	24½	25½	26½
Hip	20	21	22	23	24	26	28	30	32	34
Height	22	25	29	31	33	37	41	45	49	53

BOYS

Size	1	2	3	4	6	8	10	12	14	16
Chest	20	21	22	23	24	26	28	30	32	34
Waist	19½	20	20½	21	22	23	24	25½	27	29
Neck					11	11½	12	12½	13½	14
Hip	20	21	22	23	25	27	29	31	33	35½
Height	25	29	31	33	37	41	45	49	53	55

HOW TO ESTIMATE YARDAGE

The fabrics we sew today come in many widths. Since the space on the pattern envelope is limited, at times the fabric width chosen may not be included in the yardage chart provided for each pattern.

The Fabric Conversion Chart reprinted below was developed by Rutgers, The State University of New Jersey, Cooperative Extension Service, to help estimate the yardage for different fabric widths.

FABRIC CONVERSION CHART

FABRIC WIDTH	32"	35"-36"	39"	41"	44"-45"	50"	52"-54"	58"-60"
Yardage*	1⅞	1¾	1½	1½	1⅜	1¼	1⅛	1
	2¼	2	1¾	1¾	1⅝	1½	1⅜	1¼
	2½	2¼	2	2	1¾	1⅝	1½	1⅜
	2¾	2½	2¼	2¼	2⅛	1¾	1¾	1⅝
	3⅛	2⅞	2½	2½	2¼	2	1⅞	1¾
	3⅜	3⅛	2¾	2¾	2½	2¼	2	1⅞
	3¾	3⅜	3	2⅞	2¾	2⅜	2¼	2
	4	3¾	3¼	3⅛	2⅞	2⅝	2⅜	2¼
	4⅜	4¼	3½	3⅜	3⅛	2¾	2⅝	2⅜
	4⅝	4½	3¾	3⅝	3⅜	3	2¾	2⅝
	5	4¾	4	3⅞	3⅝	3¼	2⅞	2¾
	5¼	5	4¼	4⅛	3⅞	3⅜	3⅛	2⅞

***Add an additional ¼ yd. for wide span conversion in fabric, for nap or one directional prints, for styles with sleeves cut in one piece with body of garment.**

Reprinted courtesy of: New Jersey Cooperative Extension Service, Rutgers, The State University

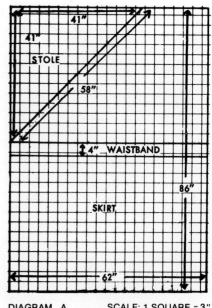

QUILT SKIRT AND STOLE

MATERIALS: 62″ × 86″ lightweight quilt (ours is patchwork design). Belting (lining) for waist, approximately 1½″ wide. Heavy duty hook and eye. 1 pkg. of bias hem facing (2″ wide, color of your choice).

TO MAKE: Measure yourself from waist to desired floor length (our 41″ is for a fairly tall girl). Using the 62″ for width of skirt, cut out desired length. Following Diagram A, cut out waistband and stole according to placement and measurement. Remove the quilting stitches and filling from the waistband piece and use only the print fabric. Gather skirt to waist size. Line waistband with belting, attach to skirt. Close with hook and eye. Bind raw edge of stole with ruffling left over from quilt or finish off with bias hem facing.

DIAGRAM A   SCALE: 1 SQUARE = 3″

FOR
MEN AND WOMEN

Celebrate the spirit! It will proclaim your love of original-
ity and excellence and fun.

Here are a cape and a coat warm as only quilts can
make them . . . a rickrack hat with a big red tassel
. . . an ultrasuede poncho graced with fallen leaves
. . . a hand-painted dress ethereal as a midsummer day
. . . a stenciled caftan trimmed with gold . . . a skirt and
shawl tufted with bowknots. Here is the classic white
coat, textured by trapunto . . . an apron with plenty of
pockets . . . and another to stencil with a Moorish tile.

QUILTED CAPE AND QUILTED COAT

SIZE: 8–16

MATERIALS: Quilt for coat is 76″ × 86″; Quilt for cape is 62″ × 86″. Cape or shawl-collar coat or robe pattern in desired size. For size 16, buy a quilt 86″ × 101″. **NOTE:** Both quilts we used are reversible.

IT IS IMPERATIVE TO FOLLOW THE PATTERN LAYOUT DIAGRAMS A AND B IN ORDER TO TAKE ADVANTAGE OF THE RUFFLED EDGINGS ON THE QUILTS.

TO MAKE: Fold quilt in half crosswise. Place each of the pattern pieces on the quilt making sure that the bottom of each piece is directed to the outside ruffled edge of the quilt which will become the bottom of the cape or coat. Adjust pattern to your length. The center back should be on the fold; the center front takes advantage of the ruffled edged down the front continuing around bottom. Join the pieces together, following pattern directions, making sure that the bottom edges match perfectly. We suggest you bind the inside seams because of the quilting.

NOTE: If you buy a reversible quilt for cape, binding the 2 inside seams with bias tape will make the cape reversible. To finish neckline for the cape, take left-over pieces of the ruffle and use it to bind the neckline the same way it bound the quilt.

SPECIAL INSTRUCTIONS FOR COAT: In order to take advantage of the edging on the collar, carefully place the collar pattern and the front of robe pattern together as shown and attach with scotch tape. This means the

collar will become part of the front and NOT a separate piece. The dotted line extention at the center back of collar shows you where to cut. This creates a very pretty shawl collar with a long point at the center back. The point should be seamed on the wrong side and sewn to the back neckline. Be sure that your sleeve pattern is directed to the outside edge of quilt to take advantage of the trim.

DIAGRAM A   62″ x 86″   CAPE

Assemble coat according to the pattern except for the special instructions for the collar.

NOTE: The **dotted lines** indicate where you should **extend** cutting lines.

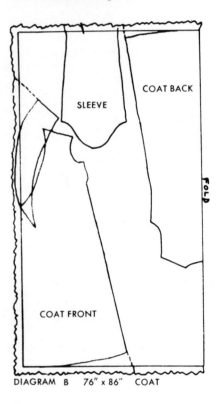

DIAGRAM B   76″ x 86″   COAT

HAT

MATERIALS: Blue felt, 14″ × 24″. Red felt, 6″ × 24″. Yellow felt, 2¾″ × 24″. Medium width rick rack in white, yellow and green (1 pkg ea). Narrow width soutache in white, yellow, red, navy and green (1 pkg ea). Red yarn for tassel.

TO MAKE: Enlarge Diagram 1 following di-

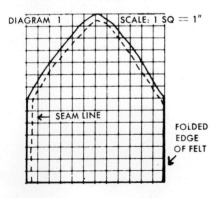

rections on page 8. Cut out pattern for hat. Fold blue felt in half, crosswise; place pattern on fold; pin and cut out hat. Turn bottom of blue felt up ½″. Place red felt band on top, leaving ¼″ of turned blue felt showing at lower edge. Stitch along both edges of red felt. Cut yellow felt into two lengthwise strips, one 1″ wide, the other 1¾″ wide. Cut one edge of 1″ yellow strip in zigzag pattern (Diagram 2). Place both yellow strips on the red band, spacing as in Diagram 2; stitch along edges of both strips. (**NOTE:** Stitch directly below zig-zag on the 1″ strip.) Stitch rick rack and soutache in place, following spacing on Diagram 2. Position two halves of hat with right sides together; stitch ½″ seam along side and crown. Turn hat right-side out.

TASSEL: Cut piece of cardboard 7″ long and wind red yarn around it 25 to 40 times, depending on desired fullness. Draw a doubled yarn strand, 10″ long, under strands at one end of cardboard and tie securely. Cut

strands at opposite end. Tightly wrap a strand of yarn several times around top of tassel, ½″ to 1″ below tie; knot. Sew to hat.

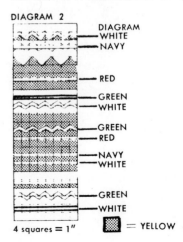

You might make each item in another fabric and utilize Ultrasuede for trim, or if you make the items in Ultrasuede, check your scraps for interesting textures to use as appliqué. Bags shown include an 11" side zipper with a hidden inner pocket, but we have simplified the instructions to include top zipper closure only.

MATERIALS: ⅞ yd Ultrasuede for each bag. 16" separating metal zipper. Fusible web ¼ yd. **Optional supplies:** Ultrasuede scraps in contrast colors. Beads with a wide hole. Shell—flat with hole in top. Feathers in natural colors. Green florist tape to wrap feathers. Metal studs for bag bottom. Heavy cardboard 6" × 16" for bag bottom.

TO MAKE: Cut pieces for bag. Main piece 30" × 17", four 25" × 1½" strips per bag for handles. Use pattern A to cut 2 side in-sets: enlarge to twice size shown and cut on fold to get full pattern piece. Sew zipper to main piece along the 17" edges. Stitch side insets to bag with right sides together with ½" seam allowance. Fuse handle strips together with fusible web. Zigzag stitch over cut edges using a wide width and a long stitch setting. Attach handles to bag near zipper about 3" from each end. **Leaf appliqué:** Use patterns C, D or your own leaf shapes. (Our designer used an assortment of maple leafs that she had pressed between paper.) Cut out 3 different colors and arrange on bag. Use a little rubber cement or fusible web to hold in place. Do a running stitch by hand close to edge using a single strand of thread. **Feather Bird:** Cut out shape using pattern B in scraps of Ultrasuede. Sew on feathers with tiny hand stitches, beginning at tailfeathers and moving up towards head. At breast build up feathers to get a rounded, full breast. Try to arrange feathers in patches of colors. For example, our designer grouped most white feathers at neck and green feathers on the wing. Sew on a bead for eye. **Feathers and shell:** Arrange some feathers in a circle using a variety of shapes and colors. Use a little rubber cement to hold in place. Slip stitch feathers through stem with 2–3 tiny stitches to secure. Longer feathers may need an extra tack at spine center. Sew shell in center of arrangement to conceal stitching. **Streamers:** Cut ⅜" strips from 5–7" long and sew near handle base. Arrange and sew a few small feathers over it. At the end, slide bead up about 1". Group 3–4 feathers together and wrap with florist tape to hold securely. Whipstitch to end of streamer and slide bead down over stitching.

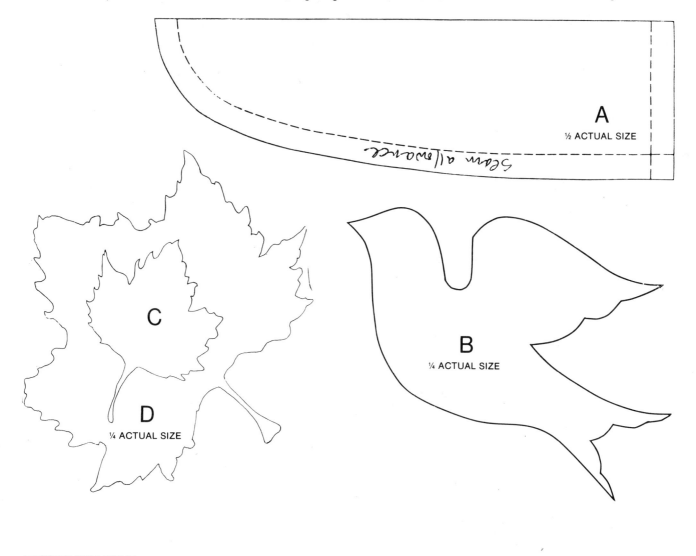

A ½ ACTUAL SIZE

Seam allowance

C
D ¼ ACTUAL SIZE

B ¼ ACTUAL SIZE

ULTRASUEDE BELT

MATERIALS: Belt buckle or closure in width of choice. Ultrasuede: 2 strips, waist measurement plus 1" × width of closure. Stiff interfacing or belting: use the same measurement as for Ultrasuede. Feathers: about 20 shown. Rubber cement.

TO MAKE: Place interfacing or belting in between two layers of Ultrasuede. Use a wide zigzag stitch over side raw edges. Insert into belt closure and adjust to fit waist. Whip-stitch ends in place. Arrange feathers along each side of buckle. Use a little rubber cement to hold while taking a few tiny stitches to secure. Give a few smaller feathers on top of larger ones to conceal stitches.

WOMAN'S PONCHO

The pattern is for an unlined poncho, though we've shown it lined for added warmth. Purchase the amount of yardage required in each of your fabric choices. You might make each item in another fabric and utilize Ultrasuede for trim, or if you make the items in Ultrasuede check your scraps for interesting textures to use as appliqué.

MATERIALS: Pattern in desired size. Feathers. Florist tape. Beads: 12 large ones for neck opening, 18 small ones for streamers and birds' eyes. Ultrasuede or other contrast scraps in 6 colors. Rubber cement.

TO MAKE: For lined poncho: Cut 2 ponchos with pockets in lining fabric only. Cut 16 streamers 3/8" wide from 12"–20" long.

Baste to front of poncho, varying the lengths to please you.

Leaf appliqué: Use patterns C, D or your own leaf shapes. (Our designer used an assortment of maple leafs that she had pressed between paper.) Cut out 3 different colors and arrange on bag. Use a little rubber cement or fusible web to hold in place. Do a running stitch by hand close to edge using a single strand of thread.

Feather Bird: Cut out shape using pattern B in scraps of Ultrasuede. Flip pattern to get one going in the other direction. Sew on feathers with tiny hand stitches, beginning at tailfeathers and moving up towards head. At breast build up feathers to get a rounded, full

breast. Try to arrange feathers in patches of colors. Sew on a bead for eye. Stitch each poncho separately and then join. Sew hood area first, turn and then sew outer edges. Use a wide zigzag stitch over edges to hold flat. Slide bead up streamers about 1". Group 3–4 feathers together and wrap with florist tape to hold securely. Whipstitch to end of streamer and slide bead down over stitching.

Neckpiece: Use buttonhole twist to string large beads, alternating with feathers that have been wrapped with florist tape. At the center stitch several groups of feathers together to a scrap of Ultrasuede. Wrap with florist tape as needed to hold firmly and then sew through the tape to secure.

MAN'S PONCHO

SIZE: Fits all sizes—Small, Medium, Large.

MATERIALS: 1¾ yds Ultrasuede. Contrast color scraps Ultrasuede. 2 yds cording. Rubber cement or fusible web.

TO MAKE: Follow Diagram and mark measurements directly on fabric with tailor's chalk or pencil. Do appliqué first. Use rubber cement or fusible web to hold it in place. Then

do a running stitch by hand with one strand sewing thread close to outer edges of each appliqué piece. Sew side seams. Turn under ½" at neckline and sleeve edges and use a wide zigzag stitch to hold edges flat. You may also want to use a little rubber cement or fusible web before stitching. Casing: Turn up 1½" at hem and zigzag stitch at top and lower edges. Make 2 narrow slits at center front and pull drawstring through. Knot ends.

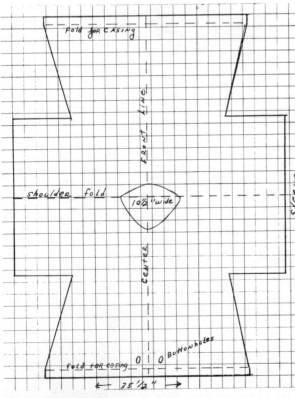

SCALE: 1 SQUARE = 2"

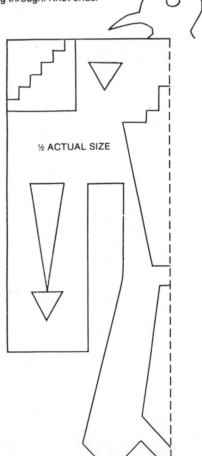

½ ACTUAL SIZE

PATCHWORK COAT

SIZE: Can be made in pattern sizes 8–16.

MATERIALS: Jacket pattern in desired size. Patchwork fabric made from a variety of fabrics (we used 3 wool tweeds and cotton satins in 3 shades of yellow, 1 shade of brown, 1 shade of beige and 1 print). Fabric for sleeves and facings. Lightweight fabric for backing patchwork. Batting.

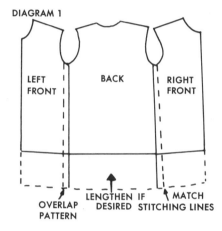

DIAGRAM 1

TO CUT: To avoid matching and to eliminate bulkiness, side seams of coat have been eliminated, and coat is cut in one piece. To do this, first make a duplicate of front pattern piece; then lay out pieces for right front, left front and back on a flat surface. Tape fronts to back at side seams, matching **stitching** lines (Diagram above).

FENCEPOST QUILTING

TO MAKE: Strips for patchwork coat are cut from fabrics of varying textures and patterns (see photo). Make enough patchwork fabric to accommodate right front, left front and back pieces of sewing pattern (Diagram above). Make an actual size pattern 2½" × 7½" for strip (this measurement includes ¼" seam allowance all around). Make a sandpaper pattern by drawing the rectangu-

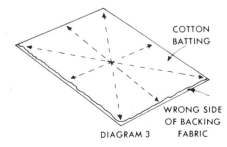

DIAGRAM 3

lar outline on artist's tracing paper and pasting onto the smooth side of sandpaper; cut out exactly on the drawn lines. When cutting fabric strips, place rough side of sandpaper on fabric to prevent pattern from slipping. Or, make a cardboard or illustration board stencil. This quilting is a zig-zag pattern, and accuracy in cutting and joining is essential. If there is any doubt about color fastness, or if there is a possibility of shrinkage, wash and iron the fabric before beginning to work. If the fabric for the quilting top is washed, also pre-shrink the fabric for the back. Determine the size you need and cut the number of strips required. Check photo for color arrangement. Each long strip is a combination of two colors; these should be joined before assembling. Strips may be trimmed off at the edges after sewing. When top has been completed, cut fabric for back slightly larger than top all around. Cut batting to same size as backing fabric. Place batting on wrong side of backing, and fasten two layers together with long hand-basting stitches: begin in center and sew toward outer edge until there are a number of diagonal lines as shown in Diagram above. Center top of quilting over batting; baste together diagonally as before. Quilting can be done either by hand or by machine. To determine proper tension and stitch length for machine quilting, test on scraps of fabric and batting before working on quilt. We suggest using matching thread when quilting colored fabrics as it makes the small stitches appear even smaller. When quilting has been completed, cut out coat in one piece, lengthening if desired, and proceed according to pattern directions. Fit by taking up fullness in underarm darts.

QUILTED COAT WITH CROCHETED SLEEVES

MATERIALS: Coat pattern in desired size. Amount of coat fabric indicated on pattern envelope. ¾ yd of 45″ patterned accent fabric for yoke inset, cap sleeve and coat bottom border. 1 yd 45″ solid color fabric to make bias strips of fabric binding for yoke and border trim and all binding and tie trim.

TO MAKE: If doing your own quilting, cut coat 1″ larger than pattern. Use a light polyester batting. Quilt from center out. Recut fabric to fit pattern. Cut center front yoke out of desired patterned accent fabric per Diagram A. Baste to right front. Quilt from top to bottom. Leave yoke edges raw; they will be covered with bias fabric binding. Stitch coat center back seam, if coat has one. From patterned accent fabric, cut bottom border for coat: measure up 11¼″ from bottom of pattern. Cut two. Sew border back seams together. Baste to coat bottom over coat fabric. Quilt border fabric from top to bottom. Leave top edge of border raw; it will be covered with bias fabric binding. To make solid color bias fabric binding for yoke, border and all trim, cut 1½″ wide strips on the diagonal. Sew strips together to form 10 yds. total. Turn under ⅛″ on both edges. Press. **(NOTE:** When stitching fabric bias binding to coat work as close to edge as possible.) Take 20″ of bias fabric binding; fold in half. Press. Sew on top of front yoke raw edges mitering at lower left corner. Take 60″ of bias fabric binding; fold in half. Press. Sew on top of raw edge of bottom coat border. Stitch fronts of coat to back at shoulders, etc., continuing to end of pattern directions. Cut sleeve cap per Diagram B. Cut one piece of coat fabric, 1 of patterned accent fabric for each sleeve. With right sides together, stitch around sleeve caps. Leave 1″ for turning. Trim edges, turn. Blind stitch opening. Press. Starting at shoulder seam, center cap under bias fabric trim. Blind stitch in place. Cap **will not** extend to underarm. Sew crochet sleeve to armhole.

SLEEVES AND HAT

SIZES: Directions are for size 6–8. Changes for sizes 10–12 and 14–16 are in parentheses. **Hat:** One size fits all.

MATERIALS. Brunswick Aspen (2 oz.) skeins.

Sleeves: 4 (5–6) skeins. **Hat:** 2 skeins. Crochet Hook Size K (or size to obtain gauge.)

GAUGE: 5 sts = 2″.

SLEEVES: Ch 28(31–34). **Row 1:** Sc in 2nd ch from hook and each ch across, ch 1, turn. **Row 2:** Working in back loops only, sc in each sc across, ch 1, turn. 27(30–33) sc. Rep Row 2 for pat. Work to 18″ from beg or desired length to underarm.

SHAPE CAP: Row 1. Sl st across first 3 sts, sc in each st to last 3 sts, ch 1 turn. **Row 2:** Sk first sc (1 sc dec), sc in each sc to last sc, do not work in last sc, ch 1, turn. 19(22–25) sc. Rep Row 2 every row 3(4–5) times, every other row 4 times. Fasten off.

FINISHING: Sew sleeve seams. From right side join yarn to one outer edge of underarm. Being sure to keep work flat, work 1 row sc evenly around entire sleeve cap, ending at outer edge of other underarm. Fasten off. Block. Sew sleeve to armhole.

HAT: Beg at center top ch 4, join with a sl st to form ring. **Rnd 1:** Ch 2(counts as first hdc), work 11 hdc into ring, **DO NOT JOIN.** Mark beg of rnds. 12 hdc. **Rnd 2.** Working in back loops only hdc in top of ch-2,* 2 hdc in next hdc, hdc in next hdc, rep from * around, end 2 hdc in last hdc, 18 hdc. **Rnd 3:** Hdc in first hdc, 2 hdc in next hdc, * hdc in each of next 2 hdc, 2 hdc in next hdc, rep from * around, end hdc in last hdc. **Rnd 4.** Hdc in first hdc,

2 hdc in next hdc, * hdc in each of next 3 hdc, 2 hdc in next hdc, rep from * around, end hdc in each of last 2 hdc. **Rnd 5:** * Hdc in each of 4 hdc, 2 hdc in next hdc, rep from * around. 36 sc. **Rnd 6:** Hdc in each of 2 hdc, * 2 hdc in next hdc, hdc in each of next 5 hdc, rep from * around, end hdc in each of last 3 hdc. **Rnd 7:** * Hdc in each of 6 hdc, 2 hdc in next hdc, rep from * around. 48 hdc. Work 2 rnds even ending last rnd sl st to first st of rnd, ch 1, turn. **Rnd 10 (wrong side):** Loop st in first st (to form loop st take a ruler, going from front to back loop yarn around ruler, insert hook in first st, and pull yarn thru, complete as an hdc, drop loop off ruler. Loop should fall to right side of work), work 1 loop st in each st around. Rep Rnd 10, 6 times more, ending last row sl st to first st. Fasten off. Cut loops. Block.

Diagram A   Diagram B

PATTERN   TOP OF
CENTER FRONT   SHOULDER FOLD

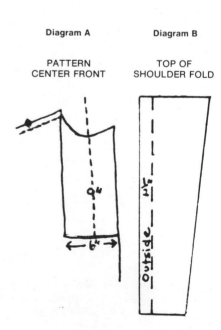

AMERICAN INDIAN PATCHWORK JACKET

Adapted from Rio Grande Pueblo Dance Costumes

MATERIALS: Jacket pattern in desired size. One yd each (for size 10) of fabric in the following colors: red, white, beige, gold, rust, turquoise, olive green and black. Fabric is also needed for jacket bands and lining. (We used the same black fabric as was used for the patchwork.) 2 frogs.

TO MAKE PATCHWORK: Five rectangles must be made for the fabric for the jacket—two rectangles for the jacket fronts (one for each side), two for the sleeves, and one for the jacket back. Follow the diagrams below for cutting the individual bands, squares and triangles that make up the patchwork. Keep in mind that the five patchwork rectangles should be made wide enough to accommodate the width of the jacket front, back and sleeve pattern pieces. Of course, this will vary from one size pattern to the other. Therefore, add or subtract extra triangles, squares, etc. where necessary. Accuracy in measurement is important in patchwork, and you may want to make cardboard pattern pieces for cutting the patches. **To all dimensions given in the Diagrams, remember to add ¼" all around for seam allowances.** Cut all triangles and squares with base on grain of fabric. Once all of the patches have been cut, stitch the patches together (match triangles and squares at seams) to create bands. Then, sew the bands together to make the five patchwork rectangles. **NOTE:** You may need to lengthen your jacket pattern to create the style photographed. Depending upon the selected pattern size and the desired jacket length, some of the bottom bands of patchwork can be eliminated. Determine the finished length of the jacket body and sleeves before cutting out the patches and sewing together the bands. Make any necessary adjustments to the dimensions given in Diagrams A and B.

TO FINISH: Cut the jacket pattern pieces from the five patchwork rectangles. Make sure that the bands of patches will match at the side seams and across the sleeves. Cut out the jacket bands and lining. Construct the jacket following the pattern instructions. Stitch the frogs to the jacket fronts.

DIAGRAM A—Patchwork for Jacket Fronts and Back

Width of Jacket Front or Back Pattern Pieces (determined by pattern size being used—add or subtract pieces where necessary)

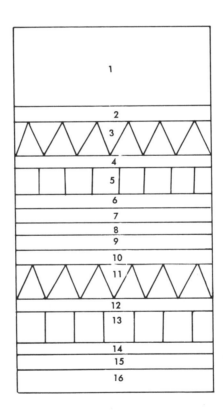

NOTE: Add ¼" all around for seam allowance! 1. beige band 8" wide. 2. black band 1¼" wide. 3. alternating rust and turquoise triangles 3½" high and 3½" wide at the base (turquoise triangles point up). 4. black band 1⅛" wide. 5. alternating red and white 2¾" squares. 6. black band 1¼" wide. 7. olive green band 1⅝" wide. 8. black band 1" wide. 9. turquoise band 1½" wide. 10. black band 1¼" wide. 11. alternating rust and gold triangles 3½" high and 3½" wide at the base (gold triangles point up). 12.

black band 1¼" wide. 13. alternating red and white 3" squares. 14. black band 1⅛" wide. 15. turquoise band 1⅜" wide. 16. black band 2¼" wide (includes 1" hem allowance).

DIAGRAM B—Patchwork for Jacket Sleeves

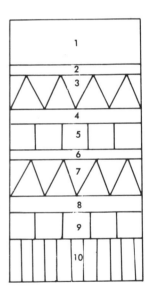

NOTE: Add ¼" all around for seam allowance! 1. beige band 4½" wide. 2. black band 1" wide. 3. alternating rust and turquoise triangles 3½" high and 3½" wide at the base (turquoise triangles point up). 4. black band 1¼" wide. 5. alternating red and white 2¾" squares. 6. black band 1" wide. 7. alternating rust and gold triangles 3½" high and 3½" wide at the base (rust triangles point up). 8. turquoise band 1¾" wide. 9. alternating red and white 2¾" squares. 10. alternating black and olive green rectangles 4¼" tall (includes 1" hem allowance) black rectangles are 1" wide and olive green rectangles are 1½" wide. Width of Jacket Sleeve Pattern Piece (determined by pattern size being used—add or subtract pieces where necessary).

APPLIQUE FOR FRONTS

DOUBLE FOLD BIAS TAPE FOR STEMS

PRINT I—YELLOW BACKGROUND CALICO

PRINT II—RED WITH YELLOW RINGS

PRINT III—RED BACKGROUND CALICO

PRINT IV—BLACK BACKGROUND CALICO

APPLIQUE FOR SLEEVES

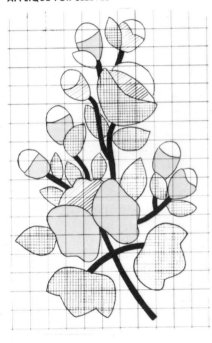

APPLIQUE FOR BACK

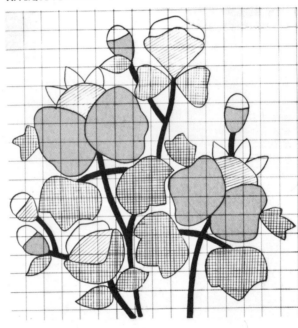

SCALE: 1 SQUARE = 1"

CHILD'S APPLIQUÉD COAT

MATERIALS: Child's coat pattern in desired size. Muslin for coat backing. 4 different calico prints for appliqués. Fabric for lining (we used one of the appliqué fabrics). Double fold bias tape. Purchased piping or bias tape and cording to make your own piping. **NOTE:** You may have to make some changes in your pattern to create a coat like ours. Our coat is lined to edge and is designed to just meet at the center front. Use the center front markings on the coat front pattern piece to determine the finished edge of the coat. **Remember to add ⅝″ to the center front for seam allowances.** To make it easier to sew the piping to the edge of the coat, slightly

round the center front corners on the pattern tissue at the neckline and hem edges.
TO MAKE: Make the necessary adjustments to the coat pattern pieces (see note above). Cut the coat fronts, sleeves, and back from muslin. Stitch darts. Enlarge the appliqué designs, following directions on page 8. Using dressmaker's carbon paper and tracing wheel, transfer the designs to the muslin coat pattern pieces to use as a guide in placement of the appliqués. The diagrams give the design for the right front and sleeve of the coat. For the left front and sleeve, reverse the design.) For appliqué pattern pieces, trace around each leaf and portion of

flower, add ¼″ all around for seam allowance, cut out. Place patterns on fabrics, cut out. With invisible slip stitches, appliqué the flowers and leaves to the fronts, sleeves, and back. Use double fold bias tape for stem appliqués.

TO FINISH: Sew appliquéd coat pattern pieces together. Using the same adjusted pattern pieces as used for the outside of the coat, cut fronts, sleeves, and back from lining fabric. Baste piping to seamlines of appliquéd coat. Stitch lining to coat, leaving an opening at the hem. Turn coat and slip-stitch opening closed.

TIE-DYED DRESS

MATERIALS: Drawstring-neck pattern in desired size. Lightweight muslin fabric in yardage designated by pattern, allowing extra for design adjustments; include yardage for scarf if desired. Rit Liquid Dye in one to five colors desired to make design; here, Fuchsia 1, Dark Green 35, and Evening Blue 27. Rit Powder Dye for background, two or more boxes depending on amount of fabric and intensity of color; here, Scarlet 5 and Chestnut Brown 43. Scissors. Straight pins. Rubber gloves. Bristle brush, medium size. Enamel, glass or stainless steel (not aluminum or iron) equipment: Measuring cup, spoon, large spoon, bowl, and pot to accommodate fabric with ease. Working surface covered with old newspapers (young ones rub off ink). Rubber bands.

TO MAKE: Wash fabric first to preshrink and remove all sizing. Let dry and iron smooth.

Fold fabric yardage in half crosswise. Lay out pattern to get some sense of where you want to place your design on the fabric. Since fabric is doubled, both pieces of the pattern will be mirror images of each other and match exactly. Keep the design simple such as the curves on our dress. If necessary, mark notations (pin or cut notches) for your design. Wet the fabric thoroughly but lay it out flat and smooth on newspapers. When using dyes, always wear rubber gloves. Usually it is best to dye with your lightest color first. According to intensity of color, mix together small parts of dye color and water. Test color by dipping small fabric strips in dye solution. Using paint brush, paint on dye following your design; take into account that the dye will spread out on the fabric slightly. After painting all design areas with that dye color, wash utensils and brush thoroughly before using the second dye color. Continue until design is complete. Roll up the fabric along the lines of the design; selvages may not be aligned. Wrap rubber bands tightly around the design area. Rinse hot water over the design area until no excess dye runs out. After following directions for dissolving Rit powder dye, pour dye in pot of simmering water. Put rolled up fabric into dye pot. Let simmer for at least half an hour or more until desired color is obtained. Remember, when dry, fabric will be at least one shade lighter. Remove fabric from the pot and immediately rinse in cold water. Remove the rubber bands while the fabric is rinsing. Continue to rinse until all the excess dye has run out. Lay fabric flat on newspaper until dry. When dry, press. Lay out pattern according to directions. Sew dress according to pattern directions.

½ ACTUAL SIZE

TIE-DYED AND PAINTED DRESS

It's a good idea to do some experimenting with your scraps of fabric to see how you like various effects. And as you work on your dress, it's a good idea to do a little at a time instead of doing all the painting or dyeing at once.

MATERIALS: Pattern in desired size. Fabric that will "take" dye and paint with good results. Silk and nylon 50/50 blend crepe de chine works very well. Vogart Ball Point Paint Tubes: 1 each of gold, yellow, green, forest green, white and red. Liquitex® acrylic paints: burnt umber, Modular® yellow-green value 7, phthalocyanine green and blue, permanent green light, Acra® violet, orange, yellow and white. Rit powdered dye: 1 box of aqua. Thin rubber bands. 4 large clear plastic bags. Paintbrushes. Use a variety of fine to medium widths.

TO DYE: Cut out garment parts and stitch center front seam only. Dye each piece separately. Our designer dyed each piece at a different time to give her a chance to play

with different folds that resembled tree foliage. It's not necessary to mix all the dye at once and you can store it in a jar and reheat it when you're ready to use it again. Use thin rubber bands and try folding the dress accordion style, as shown, using 3–4 rubber bands per fold. Use color photo as a guide for additional details. When dyeing pieces, place portion not being dyed into large plastic bag and tie tightly with string. This keeps the dress from getting soiled or spattered. Follow package directions for dyeing. Rinse and let each piece dry before handling.

TO PAINT: Work on a flat surface with paper towels under fabric to absorb any excess. 1) Outline motifs using Vogart paint. This will help to keep the acrylic paints from bleeding. We've included several motifs which you can adapt for additional ones. Again, use photo as a placement guide. 2) Use acrylic paints to fill in motifs, adding water to get a softer color. Go over areas to get a richer effect. 3) Use Vogart paints for finer details and adding wispy leaves and grass.

TO FINISH: Sew dress according to pattern directions.

FOLDING FOR TIE-DYEING

STENCILING

The following are general instructions for cutting your own stencils:

MATERIALS: Textile paint for fabrics. Turpentine for cleaning brushes and stencils and as a thinner. Stiff brushes. Stencil paper or lightweight cardboard. Paper towels for cleaning. Newspaper to cover work area. Small jars or saucers to mix paints. Small wooden spoons or kitchen knives for mixing colors. Pencils. Ruler. Masking tape. Utility knife or single edge razor blade. Shellac.

TO CUT STENCILS: Draw design on stencil paper (or substitute a lightweight cardboard stencil which will need a thin coat of shellac before use.) Cut away areas to be colored with a utility knife. Use a board or several layers of newspapers to protect work area. If design areas are simple and spaced apart, one stencil can be used for several colors, keeping a brush reserved for each color. In general it is best to cut a separate stencil for each color desired.

TO STENCIL: It is a good idea to make a trial print on scrap material. Use masking tape to secure the stencil to the surface to be decorated. The surface to be stenciled should be free of oil, wax and grease. It should not be too slippery. Your paint should be of a rather cream-like consistency; however, different surfaces require different consistencies, so you must experiment. Do not have too much paint on your brush (remove excess on paper towels before applying to surface). If your brush is too filled with paint it will run under the stencil at the edges and produce a messy look. When filling in the stencil, hold your brush upright and dab or rub the paint on until the area is filled, gradually building up the desired color. Occasionally move the brush from edges of opening towards the center. Remove stencil and let dry. Stencils should be kept clean so that they do not cake-up with paint around the edges; clean with turpentine and paper towels. Stenciling can be detailed and careful like the small patterns on the chair or free and fluid like the random curves on the caftan. Experiment with things around you that will make stencils, things such as paper doilies, gummed stars, notary seals, scraps of lace, rick rack, perforated cardboard packing parts, masking tape, etc. Masking tape is especially good. Stripes, geometric designs and an endless variation can be made with its various widths. Just press it down and brush on the paint in between these strips. To make a checkerboard design, place tape on a broad working surface. Measure and cut squares with utility knife. Peel up squares and place on surface to be stenciled. Apply paint; in this design it is easier to let paint dry before removing tape.

STENCILED DIRECTOR'S CHAIR

The directors chair was done with masking tape stencils. Apply masking tape to the seat and back of the chair as per Diagrams. Paint in desired colors. Let paint dry and remove tape.

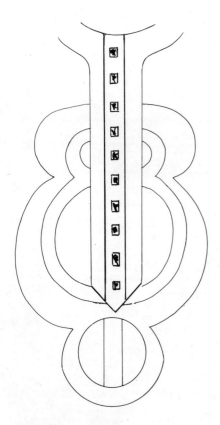

STENCILED CAFTAN

MATERIALS: Pattern in desired size. Off-white natural colored duck fabric. Braid trim. Materials listed on page 31.

TO MAKE: All stenciling and hand painting was done after the caftan was completed according to pattern directions. However, you may find it easier in this or other cases to decorate the pattern pieces prior to sewing them together. Make sure that you place a magazine or other protective layer between the two layers of fabric. Be sure to let each side dry thoroughly before beginning the other side. Braid trim is applied after stenciling. The neck detail was painted red; the front design was done free-hand following Diagram above, first having stenciled the circle at the base of the neck detail. To stencil this circle and those scattered on the sleeves, cut a stencil circle 2¾" in diameter. Press down ¾" masking tape through centers of circles (this will also hold stencil in place). Apply paint. When dry, fill in center stripes with color.

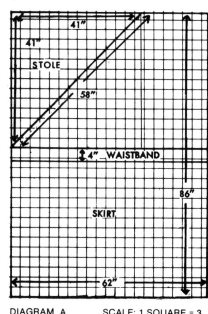

DIAGRAM A   SCALE: 1 SQUARE = 3

PRINT SKIRT AND STOLE

MATERIALS: 62″ × 86″ lightweight fabric. (Piece fabric if necessary.) 7″ skirt zipper. Hook and eye. Yarn in colors to match fabric print.

TO MAKE: Measure yourself from waist to desired floor length (our 41″ is for a fairly tall girl). Using the 62″ for width of skirt, cut out desired length. Following Diagram A, cut out waistband and stole according to placement and measurement. Sew skirt seam. Insert zipper. Gather skirt to waist size and attach to waistband. Sew on hook and eye. Add yarn tufts. **Yarn Tufts:** Cut yarn into 2″ lengths. Thread a strand of yarn through tap- estry needle, go through center of fabric de- sign and come back, place several tufts in position, knot them in place. Fold stole into triangle shape, right sides together. Sew ½″ seams, leaving a 3″ opening on one side. Turn and sew up opening. Add yarn tufts.

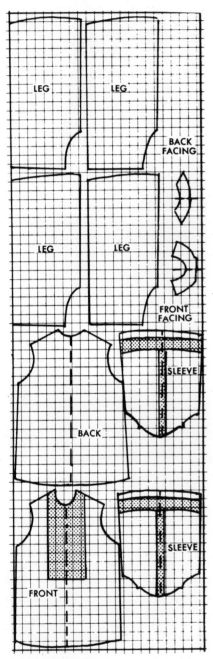

SCALE: 1 SQUARE=2″

TUNIC AND BLOOMERS

SIZE: Measurements are for medium to large. To make small size, make adjustments while assembling, not when cutting pattern pcs.

MATERIALS: 4 yds 45″ fabric. ½ yd decorative fabric trim if cut on width (¾ yd if cut on length). Ribbon trim. 1 yd elastic. 1½ yds ribbon or cording for drawstring waist.

TO MAKE: Following directions on page 8, enlarge pattern pieces. Cut them out. **Pants:**

Sew all seams. Press. Make pant leg casings; insert elastic to proper fit. Make casing at waist, leaving opening at one side for drawstring. **Tunic:** Make basting line from neckline center front to point indicated on pattern where neckline slit ends. Seam bodice front and back tog at shoulders. Cut out decorative front and back pcs and seam tog at shoulders. With right sides of bodice and decorative panel facing, seam around neck-

line ½″ and down the front ¼″ on either side of basting line coming to pt at end. Clip seams, turn, press. Turn under ½″ seam allowance on decorative panel and stitch down to bodice front and back. Apply ribbon trim at edge if desired. Seam side seams and sleeves. Set sleeves into armhole, easing at cap. Hem sleeves and bodice. Apply decorative fabric and ribbon trim. Fasten neckline with cording.

LACE APPLIQUÉ QUILT

SIZE SHOWN: 63″ × 72″ finished.

MATERIALS: Top: 4½ yds of 54″ antique white satin. Lining: 4½ yds of 54″ crepe in matching shade. Polyester quilt batting: 2 rolls or packages, 72″ × 90″. Enough lace pieces to assemble 56–9″ squares. If your antique lace supply is limited, you can seam rows of new lace trim to make squares. Lace: 36 yards of 1″ flat trim. Basting thread. Quilting thread in matching color. Quilting frame (optional).

TO MAKE: Cut and piece the satin and lining into two 72″ × 76″ rectangles. Cut or piece small items to make 56 squares of 9″ × 9″ lace. Lace should be of the same general texture and color. New pieces can be an-tiqued with a quick dip into warm coffee. Do not rinse. Stretch slightly to dry. To seam rows of new lace trim to make squares, pin strips of lace on paper just overlapping edges slightly (about ⅛″). Hand baste lace edges together going right through paper. Remove pins. Machine stitch lace through paper using 6–8 stitches per inch. Remove basting and carefully peel off paper without pulling or stretching lace. Work on as large a surface area as possible. With satin rectangle right side up, place and pin lace squares edge to edge over satin. (7 across, 8 down). Do NOT overlap or fold edges under. Edges will be concealed later with flat lace trim. Appliqué each lace square by hand to satin with tiny stitches. Remove pins. Cut lace trim into six 72″ lengths and seven 63″ lengths. Criss cross as you cover all raw edges of lace squares. Pin in place and slip stitch along both edges of lace trim catching lace squares and the satin as you stitch. Be careful not to pull or stretch lace. Reserve extra trim for finishing edges. **To quilt:** Sandwich 2 layers of batting between lace/satin top and lining. Baste the sandwich together to keep it from shifting. Trim excess batting. Quilt through the center of criss crossed lace trim with small in-and-out stitches going straight up and down through all layers. For best results, use a quilting frame (however, it isn't absolutely necessary.) Remove quilt from frame. Fold ½″ of lining and satin in towards top lace squares. Adjust and baste uneven edges. Finish by sewing remaining lace trim over raw edges around entire quilt; slip stitch both edges of lace trim border, mitering corners.

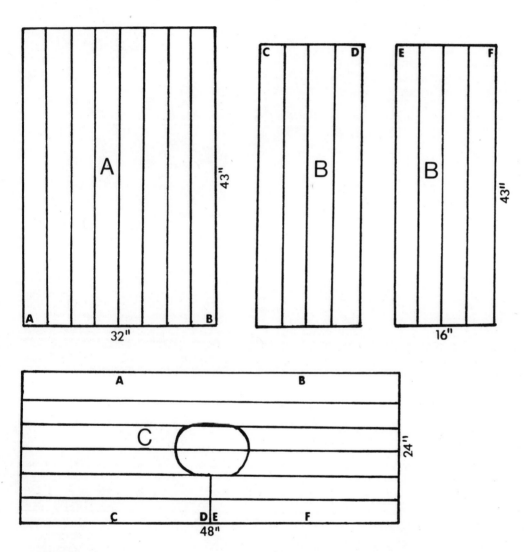

LACE CAFTAN

This loose-fitting caftan fits small to medium sizes. It can easily be adjusted by adding or reducing the number of lace strips. Make it short to the waist or knee-length for a lacy beach coverup. (Take a length measurement from under the bust to the point where you want it to end.)

MATERIALS: Lace: 26 yds of 3¾″ wide flat Cluny lace in ecru or white. Lace seam binding: 1 package. Lightweight tissue paper: approximately 6 yds—36″ wide, or Scotch tape, pieces together to get the size you need. 25″ of ribbon or cord.

TO MAKE: Make pattern with tissue paper by cutting 4 rectangles: 1 rectangle 43″ × 32″ A back; 2 rectangles 43″ × 16″ B front; 1 rectangle 48″ × 24″ C sleeves/yoke. Cut lace into sixteen 43″ lengths for sections A and B . . . and six 48″ lengths for section C. Pin strips of lace on paper just overlapping edges slightly (about ⅛″). Hand baste lace edges together going right through paper. Remove pins. Machine stitch lace through paper using 6–8 stitches per inch. Remove basting and carefully peel off paper without pulling or stretching lace. Position center of pattern C over seamed lace strips and trace

neck and front opening with a pencil on lace. Cut out opening and front slash. Assemble caftan by stitching pattern C over A and both parts of B. Place finished edge of yoke lace over raw cut edges of front and back lace sections and machine stitch. Stitch sides and underarm sleeve seams by overlapping lace edges slightly. Finish neckline, sleeve and hem raw edges with lace seam binding: stitch one edge of lace binding, fold over the edges and slip stitch remaining binding edge to the garment. Press the caftan and then fasten the neckline with either a ribbon or cord.

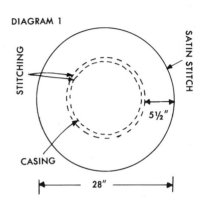

DIAGRAM 1

STITCHING

SATIN STITCH

CASING

5½"

28"

TRAPUNTO

GENERAL DIRECTIONS: The following is **important** basic information needed for making trapunto fashions. Specific instructions follow.

PATTERNS: Where specified, buy your pattern one size larger than usual to compensate for shrinkage caused by the trapunto technique.

FABRIC: Unless otherwise specified, you will need double the yardage suggested on the pattern envelope because the trapunto technique is worked between two thicknesses of fabric.

PREPARATION: Press fabric and pattern pieces smooth. Cut two of each pattern piece and label each piece.

DESIGN: Your choice of design can be original or you can copy our designs by looking at the photographs. The easiest way to create a design to your liking is to draw free hand on the actual paper pattern piece with a pencil or magic marker. Then hold the pattern piece up to your body and stand in front of a mirror to make sure that the design works well for the area where it will be used and that the proportions are right for you. With a tracing wheel and dressmaker's carbon, transfer design to fabric.

STUFFING: Stuffed areas should be light and fluffy; do not pack tightly.

TRAPUNTO TASSEL TOP

MATERIALS: 2 yds of 45″ wide unbleached muslin (for size 10). Any zig-zag sewing machine. Pattern one size larger than usual. Thread, 1 large spool of red. Cording. 1 ball butcher's string. Large-eye steel needle for pulling string through channels (you may want to use a pair of small pliers with masking tape over the pincers for pulling the needle from the channels). Stiff brush.
TO MAKE: Prepare fabric according to General Directions. Join shoulder and side seams of inside pieces, leaving opening for zipper; repeat for outside. Press. Baste inside and outside pieces together, right sides out; turn armholes and neck edges under ⅝″ and slip-stitch together. As suggested for Design under General Directions, draw a serpentine design (see photo) on pattern and transfer to **inside** of top. Machine stitch parallel lines on either side of guidelines, leaving a generous ⅜″ between, to form channel for string; use red thread and a medium-length straight stitch. You may want to experiment on a scrap first. Working on the outside of the garment, using needle and string, start threading string through channels. Pierce fabric with needle and push through channel for about 6″–8″, leaving 3″ of string at beginning. Pierce fabric with needle again, and bring needle to outside of garment. Leave a 3″-long loop and reinsert needle in same hole in channel. Temporarily, knot or pin loops so that they do not pull out as you go along. Continue until all channels are stuffed with string. Cut protruding ends and loops of string to 1″ length (there will be two ends to each hole), and fluff tassels with a stiff brush. Using a wide satin stitch, stitch ¼″ from edge around neckline and armholes. Slip-stitch bottom edges together and decorate with satin stitch. Insert zipper by hand.

TRAPUNTO HAT

MATERIALS: 1½ yds of unbleached muslin. Any zig-zag sewing machine. Red thread. Round elastic.

TO MAKE: From fabric, cut two 28″-diameter circles. Machine baste together ⅜″ from outside edges. At a point 5½″ from outside edge, make one circle of straight stitching; make another circle ⅜″ in from first to form casing for elastic. Cut elastic to size that is comfortable and insert it in casing; secure elastic and slip-stitch opening closed. Trim the brim edge with satin stitch, working over basting line (Diagram 1). Trim away excess fabric around brim up to satin stitch edging.

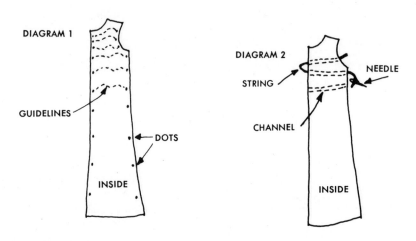

DIAGRAM 1

GUIDELINES

DOTS

INSIDE

DIAGRAM 2

STRING

NEEDLE

CHANNEL

INSIDE

TRAPUNTO COAT

MATERIALS: 12 yds of 45"-wide un-bleached muslin (for size 10). Sewing machine. Pattern, one size larger than usual (**NOTE:** We adapted a dress pattern; you just omit zipper at center back and cut two identical fronts so that finished edges of fronts will meet at center.). Thread, small spools of various colors for stitching channels. Cording, 1 ball of butcher's string. Large-eye steel needle for pulling string through channels (you may want to use a pair of small pliers with masking tape over the pincers for pulling the needle from the channels).

TO MAKE: Prepare fabric according to General Directions. On wrong sides of pieces,

measure and mark dots 1"–5" apart within seam allowances. Lightly draw guidelines across pattern piece to connect dots. Be very free when you draw these lines, and invent your own style, using wavy, zig-zag or scalloped lines or a combination (Diagram 1). Be sure side front and side back dots match. Beginning at neckline, machine stitch a parallel line on either side of each guideline, leaving a generous ⅜" between to form a channel for string; use colored thread and a medium-length straight stitch. We used the lightest color thread at the shoulder, and selected gradually darker colors as we worked downward. You may want to experiment on

a scrap first. Complete stitched design on all pieces. Working on the wrong side, with needle and string, start threading string through channels at seamline, weaving back and forth across pattern piece in a serpentine manner. Be sure that lengths of string will reach all the way across pattern piece; start new pieces of string at edges only (Diagram 2). After all channels have been stuffed with string, trim excess string from seam allowances and complete construction of garment. Bind neckline, center front edges and cuffs with bias strips of same fabric used for dress. Turn under raw edges of hem and slip-stitch together.

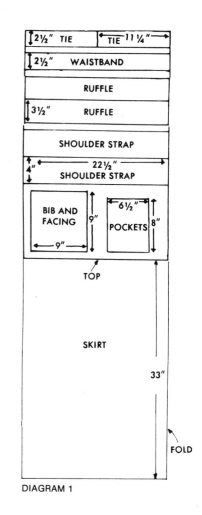

```
┌─────────────────────────────────────┐
│ ⬍2½"  TIE      │ ←─TIE─11¼"──→ │
├─────────────────────────────────────┤
│ ⬍2½"    WAISTBAND                   │
├─────────────────────────────────────┤
│             RUFFLE                   │
├─────────────────────────────────────┤
│ ⬍3½"        RUFFLE                   │
├─────────────────────────────────────┤
│          SHOULDER STRAP              │
├─────────────────────────────────────┤
│ ⬍ ←────── 22½" ──────→              │
│ 4"       SHOULDER STRAP              │
├─────────────────────────────────────┤
│ ┌────────┐      ┌─────────┐         │
│ │BIB AND │      │ ←6½"→  ↑ │         │
│ │FACING  │9"    │POCKETS │8"│         │
│ │        │      │        │↓ │         │
│ └──9"────┘      └─────────┘         │
│              ↗TOP      ↑            │
│                                      │
│                                      │
│              SKIRT                   │
│                                      │
│                          33"         │
│                                      │
│                          ↘FOLD       │
│                                      │
└─────────────────────────────────────┘
```

DIAGRAM 1

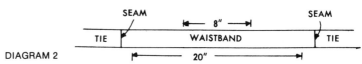

DIAGRAM 2

APRON WITH PLENTY OF POCKETS

SIZE: One size fits all.

MATERIALS: 2 yds of 45"-wide fabric. Printed fabric for pockets. Bias tape: red, yellow, lavender, black. 2 buttons.

TO MAKE: Cut pieces to sizes shown in Diagram 1 (½" seam allowance is included). Turn under ½" on top and side edges of bib and bib facing. Fold shoulder straps in half, lengthwise, right sides together. Sew one short end of each strap. Turn right side out. Turn raw lengthwise edges under ½". Pin other short end of each strap ½" below top of bib on wrong side of bib, folded edges toward center. Round off the two outside edges of ruffle at corners (see photo). Make a narrow hem along this length. Gather raw edge until it is 27" long. Starting 2" from sewn end of shoulder strap, insert gathered edge of ruffle between lengthwise edges of shoulder strap and then under side edge of bib. Pin in place. Pin bib facing to bib, wrong sides together. Top stitch ruffle to shoulder strap and bib through all thicknesses. Top stitch the top edge of bib and facing. Stitch waistband to ties and repeat for facings. With right sides together, stitch waistband to facing leaving openings shown in Diagram 2. Turn right side out. Insert bib in 8" opening in waistband and baste. Turn under ½" hem on both sides of skirt and stitch. Gather top of skirt until it is 20" wide. Insert gathered top of skirt in 20" opening in waistband and baste. Top stitch around waistband through all layers. Make 2" hem on skirt. Trim edges of pockets with bias tape; position pockets on skirt and sew around three sides. Make buttonholes in ends of shoulder straps. Try on apron, cross straps in back, and mark positions of buttons on waistband. Sew on buttons.

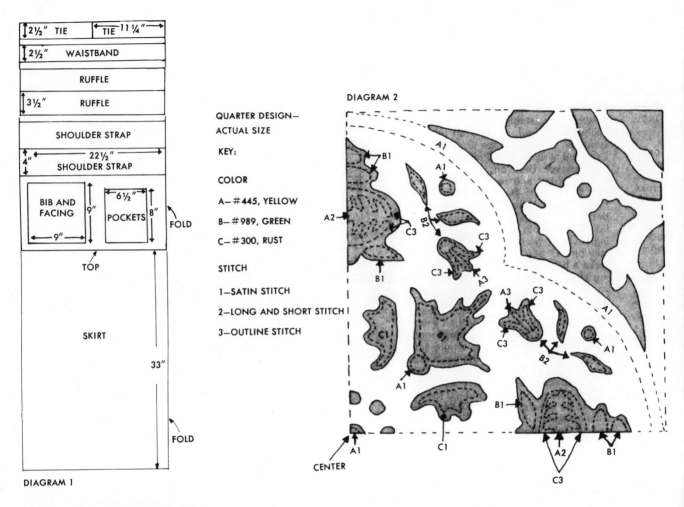

DIAGRAM 1

DIAGRAM 2

QUARTER DESIGN—
ACTUAL SIZE

KEY:

COLOR

A— #445, YELLOW

B— #989, GREEN

C— #300, RUST

STITCH

1—SATIN STITCH

2—LONG AND SHORT STITCH

3—OUTLINE STITCH

APRON WITH DECORATED BIB

SIZE: One size fits all.

MATERIALS: 2 yds of 45"-wide fabric. Six strand embroidery floss, one skn each of the following colors: yellow, green, rust. Embroidery needle. Permanent blue felt-tipped marking pen. Tracing paper. Mat knife. Heavy weight cardboard, 8" × 8". Scotchgard.

TO MAKE: Cut pieces to sizes shown in Diagram 1 (½" seam allowance is included). To make stencil for embroidery, follow solid lines, and trace Diagram 2 onto a piece of tracing paper. Leaving a ⅝" border around outside edge, place traced design in one quarter of cardboard. Transfer design from tracing paper to cardboard by using a ball point pen to outline design, scoring cardboard. Repeat three more times to complete square, placing center of design as indicated in Diagram 2 next to the quarter already transferred, matching connecting lines. With mat knife, cut out shaded areas indicated in Diagram 2 by cutting on scored lines in cardboard. Following manufacturer's directions, apply Scotchgard to bib front. Press bib, and tape to flat surface. Center cardboard over bib, and tape down. With blue marking pen, fill in areas that are cut out. Leaving blue border showing around embroidery (space between dotted and solid lines in Diagram 2), embroider bib following stitch and color key. Use three strands of embroidery floss

throughout. Turn under ½" on top and side edges of bib and bib facing. Fold shoulder straps in half, lengthwise, right sides together. Sew one short end of each strap. Turn right side out. Turn raw lengthwise edges under ½". Pin other short end of each strap ½" below top of bib on wrong side of bib, folded edges toward center. Make a narrow hem on one length and two short ends of ruffle. Gather raw edge until it is 27" long. Starting 2" from sewn end of shoulder strap, insert gathered edge of ruffle between lengthwise edges of shoulder strap and then under side edge of bib. Pin in place. Pin bib facing to bib, wrong sides together. Top stitch ruffle to shoulder strap and bib through all thicknesses. Top stitch the top edge of bib and facing. Stitch waistband to ties and repeat for facings. With right sides together, stitch waistband to facing leaving openings shown in Diagram 3. Turn right side out. Insert bib in 8" opening in waistband and baste. Turn under ½" on both sides of skirt and stitch. Gather top of skirt until it is 20" wide. Insert gathered top of skirt in 20" opening in waistband and baste. Top stitch around waistband through all layers. Make 2" hem on skirt. Turn under edges of pockets and hem; position pockets on either side of skirt and sew around three sides. Make buttonholes in ends of shoulder straps. Try on apron, cross straps in back, and mark positions of buttons on waistband. Sew on buttons.

Satin Stitch: Used to cover small background areas. Bring needle up at one edge; insert at opposite edge. Return to starting edge, carrying needle under fabric.

Long And Short Stitch: Work as satin, staggering long and short stitches. Good for shading.

Stem (Outline): For fine lines. Work left to right, inserting needle a short distance to the right and bringing to left at slight angle. For stem, keep thread below needle. For outline, keep thread above needle.

FOR THE HOME

Beauty is nice to come home to.

Here is a hammock that's ruffled and flourished with flowers . . . eyelet-edged pillows to toss on a bed in lavish disarray . . . and furniture to wrap in your favorite fabrics. Here is a flock of bluebirds bringing tulips and cherries home to bed. A quilt as sensuous as a moonlit night. Hand-painted pillows, delicate as porcelain . . . a wall hanging that's as still and bright with color as a Rousseau painting . . . a cabaña for the beach . . . and nine canvas carry-alls.

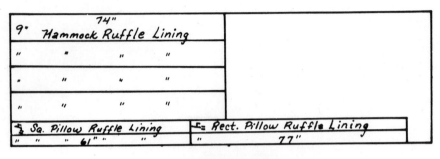

UNQUILTED GINGHAM

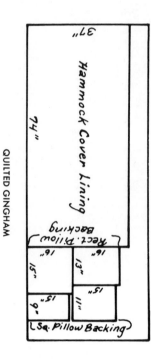

QUILTED GINGHAM

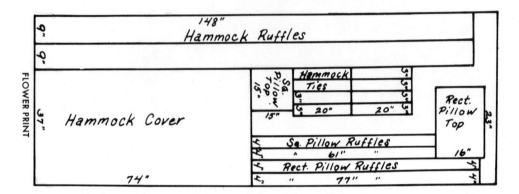

FLOWER PRINT

HAMMOCK AND PILLOW COVERS

SIZE: Hammock cover: 36″ × 73″, 8″ deep ruffle. Pillows: 15″ × 22″, 14″ square; 3″ deep ruffle.

MATERIALS: 36″ × 73″ Navy surplus canvas hammock. 4⅓ yds polished cotton floral print, 55″ wide. 3 yds quilted cotton gingham, 42″ wide. 4 yds unquilted cotton gingham, 44″ wide. 2 36″ solid brass rods. Thread. Pillow forms, 15″ × 22″ and 14″ square. **NOTE:** A ½″ seam allowance is used throughout. The cover and pillows are reversible from print to gingham. However, we refer to print side as top and gingham side as lining throughout.

HAMMOCK COVER: Ties (make 8): Right sides facing, fold each tie strip in half lengthwise and stitch long side and one end, leaving other end open. Turn right side out; press. **Ruffles (make 2):** Right sides facing, seam together 9″ ends of 2 gingham ruffle lining strips into one long piece. Repeat with print fabric. Right sides facing, seam together print ruffle strip and gingham lining strip on 2 ends and one long side. Turn right side out; press. Along remaining side of ruffle, make 2 rows of long machine stitches ½″ and ¼″ from edge for gathers using buttonhole twist in the bobbin for strength and stitching through both layers of fabric. **To Assemble:** place quilted lining piece right side up. With ruffle lining facing quilted lining (finished bottom edge of ruffle should be placed toward center of lining), gather each ruffle to fit the long sides of lining, beginning and ending ½″ from each side. Place print top right side down over lining; stitch. Turn right side out. Turn under ½″ seam allowances on open end, inserting one pair of ties at each corner (with unfinished ends inside); topstitch. To insure that cover fits Navy hammock properly, keep both ends of hammock taut by inserting solid brass rods through rope holders underneath metal eyelets, adjusting length of ropes accordingly.

PILLOW COVERS: Square: For ruffle, take 4″ × 61″ strips of print and gingham. First, seam together both ends of print ruffle strips; then, gingham lining strips, forming two circles. With right sides of circles facing, seam together one side. Turn right side out; press. Around edge of other side, make 2 rows of long machine stitches, ½″ and ¼″ from edge, stitching through both fabric layers. With print side of ruffle facing right side of 15″ square print pillow top and finished bottom edge of ruffle toward center, gather ruffle to fit top, adjusting more fullness at corners than sides; baste. For quilted gingham backing, turn under and **stitch** ½″ seam allowance on one 15″ edge of 9″ × 15″ piece. Turn under and **baste** ½″ seam allowance on one 15″ edge of 11″ × 15″ piece; turn under and topstitch a 2″ hem on basted edge. Match 2 halves of backing (each half should overlap 2″ with hemmed piece underneath—see diagram) to pillow top, right sides facing and ruffle between; stitch around all 4 sides. Turn right side out; press. Insert pillow form through slit opening in back. For **rectangular pillow cover,** follow same instructions using fabric pieces as indicated on layouts.

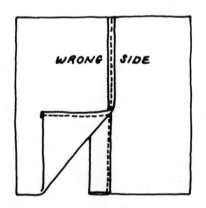

WRONG SIDE

ROUND CUSHION COVER

SIZE: 16″ in diameter, 3¾″ deep ruffle.

MATERIALS: ½ yd of quilted gingham, 42″ wide, for top and bottom. 2 yds of unquilted gingham, 44″ wide for bias ruffle.

TO MAKE: For ruffle, make a bias strip 8½″ wide and about 124″ long by piecing together as many smaller strips as necessary to get entire length from 2 yds of fabric. Leave ½″ for seam allowances. Join 2 ends, forming circle, and fold in half lengthwise, right side out. Complete round cushion cover as for square pillow cover.

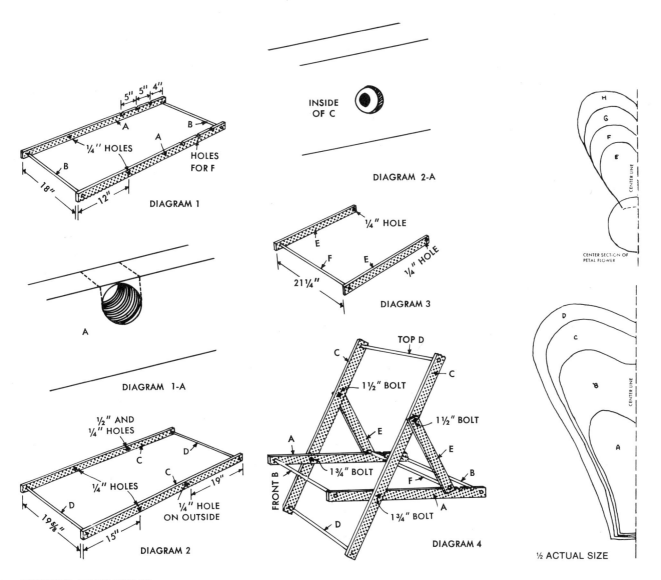

DIAGRAM 1

5" 5" 4"

A

B

¼" HOLES

A

B

HOLES FOR F

18"

12"

INSIDE OF C

DIAGRAM 2-A

DIAGRAM 1-A

A

¼" HOLE

E

F

E

¼" HOLE

21¼"

DIAGRAM 3

½" AND ¼" HOLES

D

C

C

D

¼" HOLES

D

¼" HOLE ON OUTSIDE

19⅝"

19"

15"

DIAGRAM 2

TOP D

C

C

1½" BOLT

1½" BOLT

E

A

E

B

1¾" BOLT

F

FRONT B

A

D

1¾" BOLT

DIAGRAM 4

H

G

F

E

CENTER LINE

CENTER SECTION OF PETAL FLOWER

D

C

B

A

CENTER LINE

½ ACTUAL SIZE

FOLDING DECK CHAIR

MATERIALS: For sling: 1¾ yd of No. 8 chair duck canvas or a sturdy terrycloth in color of your choice. Back lighterweight canvas and terrycloth with a second layer of canvas for strength. Hem to an 18″ width.
For Chair: 1 × 2 clear pine, cut to following lengths: two 44½″ for A, two 50″ for C, two 22″ for E. ¾″ dowels cut to following lengths: two 19½″ for B, two 21⅛″ for D, one 22¾″ for F. ¼″ stove bolts and nuts: two 1½″ long, two 1¾″ long. Eight washers for bolts. ⅝″ upholsterer's tacks. Wood glue. Basecoat and exterior paint.

TO MAKE: At center of (width of) A, bore a ¾″ diameter hole 1⅜″ from each end and a ¼″ diameter hole for bolt 12″ from front end (See Diagram 1). Make three slots to receive back support as follows: Bore a 1″ hole at points 4″, 9″ and 14″ from back end of A, placing them so edge of hole is along top edge of A; then cut from top edge of A straight down to edge of hole at widest point (Diagram 1A). Make another A in same manner. On a flat surface, assemble frame of A and B. B should fit snugly into holes in A

(sand inside of hole and end of B as needed) and apply glue to end of B before inserting. Bore two ¾″ holes in each C in same locations as for A (See Diagram 2). Bore ¼″ holes for bolts 15″ from front end of each C. On inside face of each C, at point 19″ from back end, bore a ½″ diameter hole to depth of ¼″ (to receive head of bolt, see photo). Then, using same center, bore a ¼″ hole for bolt through thickness (Diagram 2A). Assemble C and D in same manner as for A and B.
Bore a ¾″ hole 1⅜″ from one end of each E and bore a ¼″ hole for bolt 1″ from other end. Assemble E and F as before (Diagram 3).
Round off all corners on A, C and E with a wood file or sandpaper. Place frame A/B inside frame C/D and attach with 1¾″ bolts so head of bolt is on inside of A, washer is between A and C, and nut is outside of C. Attach back support with 1½″ bolts through C and E so head of bolt is recessed in ½″ hole on inside face of C, placing washers as before (Diagram 4). Apply basecoat and paint, following manufacturer's instructions.

PETAL FLOWER

MATERIALS: Scraps of firmly woven cotton fabric in bright yellow, light yellow, rose and red. Thread to match colors.

TO MAKE: Following directions on page 8, enlarge design Diagrams. Transfer the designs to the right side of your fabrics using dressmaker's carbon paper and tracing wheel: In red—5 of E and 8 of A; in rose—5 of F and 8 of B; in bright yellow—5 of G and 8 of C; in light yellow—5 of H and 8 of D and 1 circle. Prepare 8 large petals, stitching A on B, B on C, then C on D with satin stitch. Trim away extra fabric from each petal after stitching. Prepare 5 small petals in the same way. With chalk, draw a 13″ diameter circle centering it on sling's right side with top 10″ from sling's top edge. Arrange large petals within circle as shown in photograph. Appliqué them one by one. Where overlapping occurs, do not stitch portions that will be covered. Place 5 small petals in center and appliqué. Position center circle and appliqué.

STENCILED HAMMOCK

MATERIALS: Textile paint for fabrics. Turpentine for cleaning brushes and stencils and as a thinner. Stiff brushes. Stencil paper or lightweight cardboard. Paper towels for cleaning. Newspaper to cover work area. Small jars or saucers to mix paints. Small wooden spoons or kitchen knives for mixing colors. Pencils. Ruler. Masking tape. Utility knife or single edge razor blade. Shellac. 36″ × 73″ Navy surplus canvas hammock. 4¼ yds rick rack. 4¼ yds fringe.

TO CUT STENCILS: Draw design on stencil paper (or substitute a lightweight cardboard stencil which will need a thin coat of shellac before use.) Cut away areas to be colored with a utility knife. Use a board or several layers of newspapers to protect work area. If design areas are simple and spaced apart, one stencil can be used for several colors, keeping a brush reserved for each color. In general it is best to cut a separate stencil for each color desired.

TO STENCIL: It is a good idea to make a trial print on scrap material. Use masking tape to secure the stencil to the hammock, which should be free of oil, wax and grease. Your paint should be of a rather cream-like consistency; however, different surfaces require different consistencies, so you must experiment. Do not have too much paint on your brush (remove excess on paper towels before applying to surface). If your brush is too filled with paint it will run under the stencil at the edges and produce a messy look. When filling in the stencil, hold your brush upright and dab or rub the paint on until the area is filled, gradually building up the desired color. Occasionally move the brush from edges of opening towards the center. Remove stencil and let dry. Stencils should be kept clean so that they do not cake-up with paint around the edges; clean with turpentine and paper towels.

TO FINISH: Following photo, sew rick rack and fringe.

PREWORKED NEEDLEPOINT PILLOWS

MATERIALS: Each pillow is made from a preworked needlepoint canvas; choose ones with designs you love. Piping, 1 package for each pillow. Pre-gathered eyelet trim, approximately 1⅔ yds for each pillow. Pillow case backing: approximately ⅓ yd (36″ width) each of white cotton or linen fabric. Readymade pillows, 15″ × 15″ or make your own with white cotton fabric, shredded foam rubber or kapok.

TO MAKE: Centering the preworked design, mark off a fifteen inch square on the canvas. This is the guideline for the piping and trim application. Stitch the piping to the face of

continued on page 62

PREWORKED NEEDLEPOINT PILLOWS   continued from page 59

the canvas. Then stitch the pregathered eyelet. Cut two pieces for each pillow back, allowing about a 2½″ envelope overlap after hemming. Place the two hemmed pieces on front side of canvas, overlap at the midpoint, stitch on the same stitch line as used for the piping and trim. Clip, turn and press. Make and insert inner pillows. **Inner Pillows:** Cut two pieces of cotton fabric to match finished size of needlepoint, allowing ½″ extra on all sides for seam allowance. Machine stitch together, leaving 6″ opening on one side. Turn to right side and stuff. Turn seam allowance and sew up opening. Insert inner pillow. Close opening with small stitches.

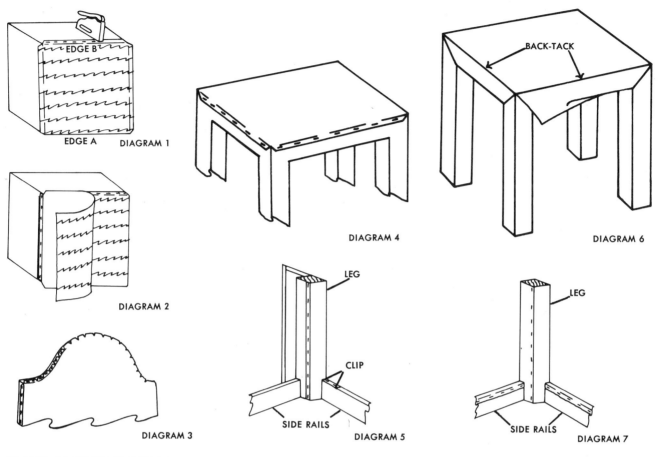

EDGE B

EDGE A   DIAGRAM 1

DIAGRAM 2

DIAGRAM 3

DIAGRAM 4

LEG

CLIP

SIDE RAILS   DIAGRAM 5

BACK-TACK

DIAGRAM 6

LEG

SIDE RAILS   DIAGRAM 7

FABRIC-COVERED FURNITURE

MATERIALS: Staple gun. Staples. Yard-stick. Pencil. Newspaper. Cardboard. Fabric in amount needed to cover your furniture (see note below). White household glue. Small pliers. New unpainted or old furniture to be revived. **(NOTE:** Begin by looking at your furniture and planning how you want fabric design to read. The design can run up and down or across.) To determine fabric yardage, measure furniture and cut a news-paper pattern to fit each section being covered. Add the extra inches needed to wrap the fabric around edges and corners. About 1″ extra all around edges of each section should be sufficient, but this can vary with the piece. Make sure paper patterns fit areas to be covered exactly. To figure yardage, lay pattern pieces out to fit within the width of the fabric you plan to buy. Measure length of layout. To allow for matching a fabric with a regular repeat design, buy ¼ to ½ yd extra depending on design's size. If you plan to make matching curtains or pillows, buy the extra yardage required.

TO MAKE: General Instructions: The fol-lowing are basic instructions for covering fur-niture and achieving a professional look. Later on, instructions are given for a few spe-cific pieces. Remove hinges, knobs and other hardware before applying fabric. First, staple fabric over edge A (see Diagram 1) of

side being covered, then staple opposite edge B instead of an adjacent side. Keep fabric taut while stapling, but avoid stretch-ing because this can distort design. Hide sta-ples, stapling in areas that won't be seen. Or, back-tack or glue as described later on. Miter corners; trim when necessary. Inside corners should be clipped so fabric can be shaped to them. Knowing when to clip, trim or miter is one of the tricks to achieving a neat, finished look. Don't hesitate to remove fabric that has been incorrectly attached, as staples can be easily removed with pliers.

Back-tacking is a good way to hide staples and a professional method for joining fabric sections. This method also achieves a straight, sharp edge. To back-tack, place wrong side of fabric along furniture edge, over edge of previously stapled fabric. Then, place a thin strip of cardboard over fabric edge. See Diagram 2. Staple through card-board and fabric. Bring fabric over cardboard and staple along opposite edge. Back-tack-ing can also be used to seam fabric on a flat side.

Edges that require only a few staples can be glued. If edge is to be finished, fold fabric to wrong side. Then, squeeze a line of glue under edge, place fabric over glue, and tem-porarily staple edge in place. When glue is dry, remove staples with pliers. To work fab-ric around curved areas, notch the curved

edge, cutting only in the allowance for fold-over. Then, glue or staple notched edge in place. See Diagram 3.

Parsons Table: Cover top, then legs and sides. Cut a rectangle of fabric to equal length and width of top plus 1″ allowance all around for stapling. Staple fabric rectangle to table top along side edges. (Refer to Gen-eral Instructions.) See Diagram 4.

Cut a fabric strip for each leg, to equal leg's length, and circumference of leg plus 1″ al-lowance all around for stapling. Starting at the inside corner, staple strip to leg. Wrap fabric around leg, clipping it where it meets side rails. See Diagram 5. Fold fabric to wrong side so that it is even with leg's bot-tom edge and meets the inside corner. Also, fold top edge even with corner edge of table top. Glue and staple fabric to bottom and top edges as instructed under General Instruc-tions. Glue and staple fabric to inside corner. Cut fabric strips for each side to equal its length plus 1″ allowance for stapling at each end, and wide enough to be wrapped around bottom edge and stapled along inside. Back-tack strips along top edge of side following General Instructions. Miter ends of strips, trimming them and turning them under. See Diagram 6. Wrap strip around bottom edge of side and staple it to the inside as shown in Diagram 7.

continued on page 66

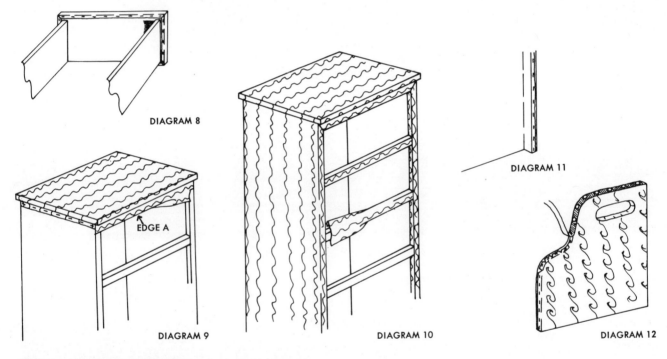

DIAGRAM 8

DIAGRAM 9

DIAGRAM 10

DIAGRAM 11

DIAGRAM 12

EDGE A

FABRIC-COVERED FURNITURE   continued from page 63

Chest of Drawers: This method works best on drawers with fronts that project out from the sides of the box like that shown in Diagram 8.

Cover drawers, top, then sides and front crosspieces. Remove all drawers. Remove knobs from each drawer. Measure length and width of drawer fronts, adding extra all around for stapling. Cut paper patterns. Cut out fabric. Staple fabric along inside of top-side of drawer front. See Diagram 8. Pull fabric tautly and staple it along inside of bottom. Miter corners. Staple sides. Measure length and width of top including amount needed to wrap around side edges, around front edge and to inside of top crosspiece. Cut paper pattern to measurements and cut out fabric. Staple fabric to sides, then back edge. Miter front corners clipping and trim-

ming as needed. At front edge A, turn fabric under crosspiece and staple along inside. See Diagram 9.

Measure height of sides adding 1″ at each end. Measure width, measuring around inside of the side front piece and add 1″ overlap for back edge. Cut pieces to these measurements. Press top and bottom edges 1″ to wrong side. Staple fabric at back edge. Glue turned edges to top and bottom. Wrap fabric around side pieces on front, clipping at corners of drawer openings. Staple fabric to inside of chest. See Diagram 10. Measure length and circumference of front crosspieces. Cut strips to equal these measurements. Cover front crosspieces with fabric strips, gluing or stapling them to inside of chest as shown in Diagram 10. Replace knobs on drawers.

Toy Chest: The following is an outline for covering this piece. Also, refer to General Instructions. Make newspaper patterns for two ends, back and front, adding about 1″ extra all around for stapling. Cut fabric from patterns. Remove lid of chest. Cut a piece of fabric large enough to wrap lid as you would wrap a flat package. Wrap lid with fabric, stapling it in place on underside. Apply fabric to back and ends, notching along curved edges and gluing and stapling notched edges in place. See Diagram 3 and accompanying instructions. To keep fabric in place along inside corners, glue and hold with a few staples. See Diagram 11. Cover edges with a novelty braid the width of the edge or slightly less than width. Use upholstery tacks to hold braid in place. See Diagram 12. Replace lid and attach hinges.

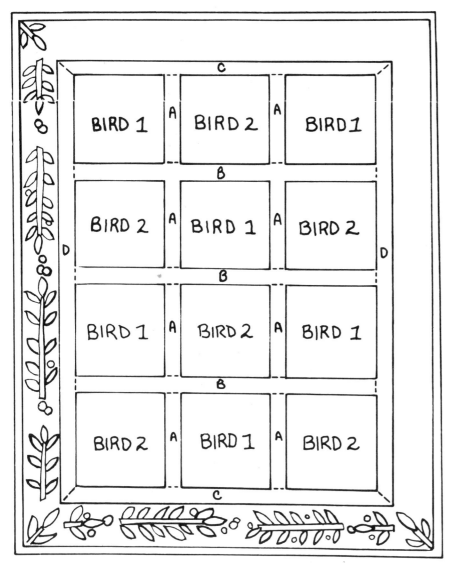

DIAGRAM 1

BIRD 1

BIRD 2

BLUEBIRD QUILT

SIZE: 73″ × 92″.

MATERIALS: Background fabric: Medium to heavy weight 36″ cotton: 4½ yds dark blue, 4¼ yds medium blue, 3 yds white, 1 yd dark pink. **Backing Fabric:** 6¼-yds medium weight 36″ cotton print for quilt backing. Buy extra fabric for dust ruffle and pillow sham ruffle to match backing. **Appliqué fabric:** Medium to lightweight solid and print cottons: 1-yd green; ½-yd light green; 1-yd assorted reds; ½-yd each of pink, light blue, peach, mustard, yellow, other desired solids, prints, checks. **Filling:** One 81″ × 96″ roll of polyester batting. Medium-fine sandpaper. Pencil. Scissors. Straight pins. Thread.

TO CUT BASIC BACKGROUND PIECES: Quilt: Blocks: 12 dark blue squares, 18″ × 18″. Medium blue lattice: A—8 strips, 3¼″ × 19¼″; B—3 strips, 3¼″ × 1⅔ yds; C— 2 strips, 3¼″ × 2 yds; D—2 strips, 3¼″ × 2⅓ yds. Border: Cut 2 strips white 7″ × 2¾ yds, 2 strips white 7″ × 2 yds. Backing: Cut 3 lengths of print, each 73″ long; seam to-

gether to form rectangle. **Pillow shams:** Cut 2 dark blue pieces 22″ × 27″, 4 medium blue lattice strips 3¼″ × 22½″, 4 medium blue lattice strips 3¼″ × 27″. Cut 4 medium blue backing pieces 17½″ × 27″.

TO CUT APPLIQUÉ PIECES: Bird blocks: For each of the 12 blocks, cut 1 body, bill, eye, shoulder, wing, breast and 2 tail feathers. For Bird 1, cut 1 branch, 3 or 4 cherries, 2 or 3 leaves. For Bird 2, cut 2 or 3 leaves, 1 shoulder piece, tulip, tulip lining and a strip of green for stem 1″ wide × 12″ long. You may wish to vary the basic design by eliminating the wing and putting in the shoulder and shoulder piece as shown in Diagram for Bird 2. For white borders, cut about 100 assorted size leaves in various shades of green, 50 cherries and 12 pieces of green stem 1″ × 17″. In general, use blues and whites for birds on cherry boughs, pinks and oranges for birds on tulips. **Pillow shams:** Cut 2 additional sets of Bird 2.

TO APPLIQUÉ: Following directions on page 8, enlarge designs. Transfer the designs to medium-fine sandpaper using

dressmaker's carbon paper and tracing wheel. Cut pattern pieces from sandpaper. You will need several sandpaper patterns for each pattern piece as they should be replaced when the edges are no longer smooth. On right side of fabric, with sandpaper pattern rough side down (roughness prevents pattern from slipping), outline your pattern piece with a sharp pencil; make several such outlines on a single piece of fabric. In other words, if you want 4 peach colored wings, draw all 4 at once, SPACING THEM AT LEAST ½″ APART. Then machine stitch on the penciled outlines (this will be the turning edge). Cut out pattern pieces with sharp scissors LEAVING A ¼″ MARGIN ALL AROUND STITCHED OUTLINES. Clip into this ¼″ seam allowance on all curved edges and at corners.

Turn in seam allowance just **inside** machine stitching; press flat. Pin and baste appliqué pieces on background fabric, following Diagrams for Bird 1 and Bird 2. Slip-stitch piece by piece, all around, with tiny invisible stitches.

continued on page 70

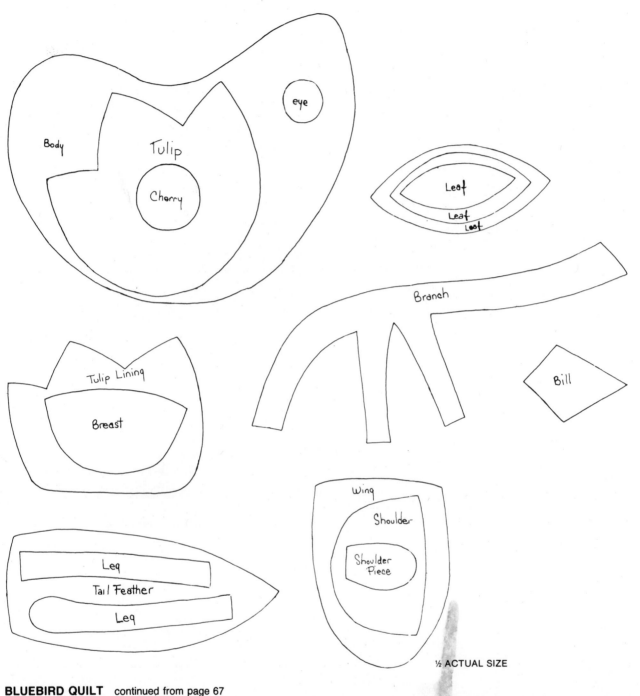

Body

Tulip

eye

Cherry

Leaf
Leaf
Leaf

Branch

Tulip Lining

Breast

Bill

Wing

Shoulder

Shoulder Piece

Leg

Tail Feather

Leg

½ ACTUAL SIZE

BLUEBIRD QUILT continued from page 67

TO ASSEMBLE QUILT TOP: Following Diagram 1, stitch together 3 bird blocks and 2 lattice strips (A) to form one horizontal panel. Make 3 more panels. To join the 4 panels, stitch together with the 3 horizontal lattice strips (B). Add lattice strips (C) at top and bottom; lattice strips (D) at sides, mitering corners. White borders: Following Diagram 1, appliqué 4 cherry sprigs on each side (2 long and 2 short); the length should vary in proportion to the side being appliquéd. Place sprigs so that they grow from corners, meeting at the center. A sprig can be appliquéd to each mitered corner after joining. Use various shades and sizes of green leaves as desired, placing cherries at random. Press

all seams open.

QUILTING: Place the backing smoothly on the floor, right side down. Lay the filling in the exact center of the backing and add the finished top, right side up. Pin the edges of the three parts on one end and one side. Start at the center of the quilt and baste a row each way to the pinned edges. Returning to the center, baste to the other sides a row at a time each way. Do not leave more than four inches unbasted and do not use too long a basting stitch. Before starting to quilt, loosen the tension on your machine and set the stitch to 6 stitches to an inch. Start from the center and machine quilt around the ap-

pliquéd parts of the bird. Then do the straight line machine stitch quilting around the center lattice work. DO NOT PULL the quilt through the machine, guide it gently. Be sure that the foot is not working the top or bottom of the quilt out of position. Too much tension will pull the bottom more than the top and you will end up with uneven edges and a lot of puckers on the back of your quilt. For edge, cut 1-yd dark pink in bias strips 1½" wide. Join and machine stitch to right side of quilt; bring to back; fold and blind stitch to back.

PILLOW SHAMS: Appliqué bird blocks so that birds face each other. Each has a 2-piece backing with an overlapped opening for insertion of pillow.

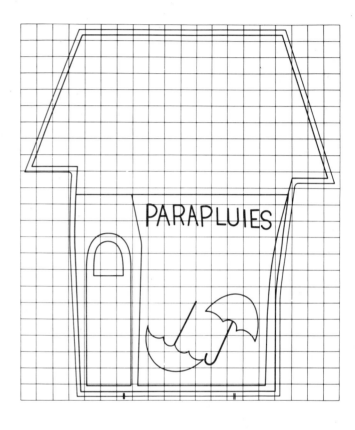

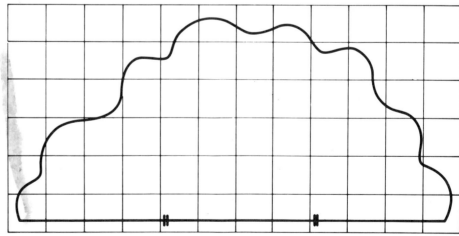

SCALE: 1 SQUARE = 1″

PILLOW VILLAGE

SIZE: Approximately 21″ high and 17″ across at widest point of roof.

MATERIALS: Sturdy fabrics such as denim, broadcloth, sailcloth (two pieces for each pillow; we used pieces 24″ × 20″). Scraps of various colors and textures of fabrics. Zigzag sewing machine. Polyester fiberfill stuffing. Thread.

TO MAKE: Following directions on page 8, enlarge designs. Trace pattern pieces from enlarged drawings and cut out of desired fabric. (Use one solid piece of fabric for pillow front and one for pillow back—cut both out at once to insure uniformity of size—the smaller pieces will be appliquéd to the pillow front fabric. Pin small pieces to background
continued on page 74

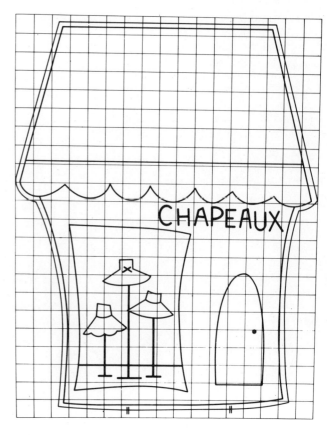

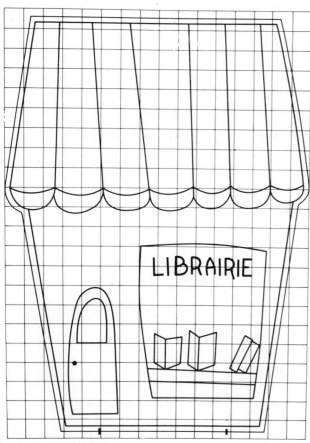

SCALE: 1 SQUARE = 1"

PILLOW VILLAGE   continued from page 71

fabric and baste in place by hand. Location of lettering may be marked with dressmaker's carbon paper. Experiment with width and tension of zig-zag stitch on scrap fabric; then proceed to zig-zag all outlines of design. Lettering is done with machine satin stitch, as are hat stands on Chapeaux pillow, umbrella handles on Parapluies, shelves on Patisserie and Fleurs, and outlines on Poissonerie porthole. Attach any auxiliary pieces by hand (ribbon on Chapeaux, button doorknobs). With right sides facing, straight stitch front and back together, leaving opening at bottom for stuffing. Stuff and close opening with whipstitch.

FULL MOON VELVET QUILT

Read instructions through carefully before starting. You may see ways to combine steps and save time.

SIZE SHOWN: 75″ × 89″ (finished).

MATERIALS: Polyester batting: 2 rolls, 81″ × 96″. Rayon velvet: 9 yds unfinished velvet, 39″–40″ wide from selvage to selvage. Fabric for backing: 9 yds. Silver lamé fabric: 1 yd. Fusible interfacing: 4 yds. Rit dyes: 1 Chestnut brown, 2 Royal Blue, 1 Gray, 1 Orchid, 1 Golden Yellow, 1 Purple, 1 Dark Green, 1 Kelly Green, 1 Orange, 1 Black, 1 Wine. Embroidery thread: 1 skein each of orange, yellow and gray. Wooden dowels: small ones for stirring dye baths. One large one or broom handle to use for wrapping quilt while dyeing.

TO CUT: As you cut, it's a good idea to label or letter code each piece with an indelible laundry marker. **A**–Pink Sky—90″ × 40″. **B**–Blue Sky—2 pcs. 35″ × 30″. **C**–Blue Border—92″ × 14″. **D**–Gray Border—92″ × 21″. **E**–Gray Rings—28″ × 30″. **F**–Silver—1½″ wide—29″ diameter. **G**–Stripes—45″ × 30″. **H**–Blue Quilt Back—2 pieces 82″ × 40″, 1 piece 42″ × 40″. **Appliques:** Cut the following fabric sections from the remainder of main pieces labeled. After dyeing, you will cut into appropriate shapes. **I**–Blue leaves—Two 35″ × 10″ pieces (B). **J**–Blue stems—28″ × 10″ (E). **K**–Green leaves—38″ × 40″. **L**–Light green leaves—92″ × 5″ (C & D). **M**–Green leaves on gray border and large green leaf in lower left corner—45″ × 10″ (G). **N**–Birds—5 pieces 12″ × 12″. **O**–Morning glories—12″ × 12″. **P**–White clouds—20″ × 40″.

TO DYE: See dye package for different dyeing methods and general manufacturer's instructions. In addition, our designer suggests these following tips: Test colors on scraps before dyeing entire sections. Colors dry lighter than when wet. Whenever you have a color that particularly pleases you, dye some extra scraps to use later for flowers, birds, etc. **(NOTE: The rayon fabric takes the dye in ways that may surprise you. To get intensities of one color, simply take pieces out of dye bath at different times.)** Dissolve powdered dye in glass jar with small amount of very hot water. Add dye solution to water container and stir before adding fabric. Always wet fabric pieces first in hot, mildly soapy water before immersing into dye bath. It's extremely important to check nap direction before dyeing. All pieces should have nap running down. You might mark the top with a safety pin or laundry marker. Rinse each piece thoroughly in cold water until water runs clear. For best results, dry each piece separately in dryer to fluff up nap. Use old towels to absorb excess moisture first. **Pink Sky (A):** Use 2 tablespoons Chestnut Brown to make dye solution. Fill bathtub with 4″–6″ of very hot water. Fold wet piece A in half lengthwise (90″ × 20″) putting wrong sides together so nap is outside. Pour small amount of dye solution into

tub water. Immerse entire piece in dye bath so that it takes on a pale shade of pink. Holding fabric along a 20″ side, wrap about 18″ around broom handle or dowel. This will protect it from being dyed any darker and will allow you to obtain a gradually shaded effect from light pink to dark orange. Add more dye solution and dye remaining 72″ slightly darker, trying to make a gradual change. Continue wrapping dyed sections around dowel and adding more dye solution so tub water gets darker and amount of fabric gets less. **Blue Sky (B) 2 pieces:** Make dye solution with 2-3 tablespoons of Royal Blue in small quantity of very hot water. Bring at least 10″ of water to a simmer in a large pot. Add small amount dye solution to obtain pale blue. Do both pieces identically. Hold fabric along 30″ side and dip in dye, making the entire piece light blue, shading to white near your hands. Add more dye and dip only the bottom ⅔, add more dye and dip just the bottom ⅓ to achieve a deep blue. **Blue Border (C) and Quilt Back (H):** Fill washing machine or large galvanized tub with very hot water. Dissolve 1½ packages Royal Blue in

small quantity hot water. Add to tub water and stir well. Immerse entire piece in dye bath so that it takes on a pale shade of pink. Holding fabric along a 20″ side, wrap about 18″ evenly. Dye blue leaves and stems (I,J) in same dye bath. **Gray border (D) and Rings (E):** Mix a dye solution with ½ teaspoon of each dye: Gray, Orchid, Brown. Add to large pot of simmering water. Test color, adding more dye if necessary, or more water if shade is too dark. **Stripes:** Cut varying widths from piece G. Dip in nine different colors using different intensities of colors you particularly like. Our designer used Chestnut Brown (to yield Orange and 3 shades of Rose), Orchid, Purple, Gray, Blue, Dark Green, Golden Yellow. **Cloud Dots:** Dye at the same time you do yellow stripes. Later cut into circles from 1½″–2¼″ **Leaves:** You can dye pieces for leaves on border (M) and large leaf in lower right corner at the same time you dye stripes. For the tall green leaves use Kelly Green for darker leaves and add Golden Yellow to Kelly Green for Chartreuse leaves. **Birds:** Use 12″ × 12″ pieces (N): Bluebirds: Mix Royal

continued on page 78

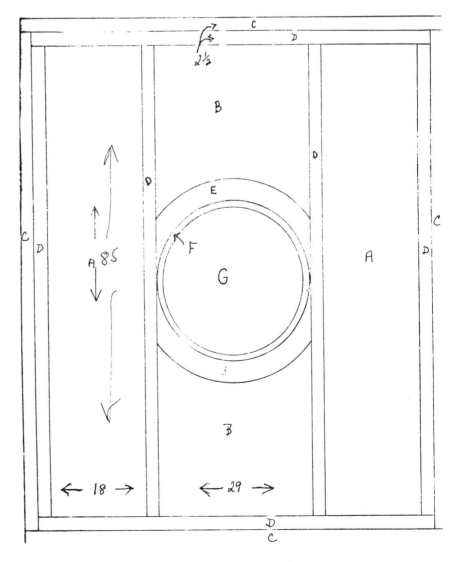

75

FULL MOON VELVET QUILT   continued from page 75

Blue and Kelly Green to get turquoise. Dye 3 pieces a different intensity of same color. Blackbird: Dye one deep Black. Maroon and Yellow Bird: Dye one with Wine mixed with a little Dark Green. **Bird's Breasts:** Use a 8" × 8" scrap. Dip in Orange, shading if you wish. Dye a small scrap deep orange for triangular patches on Blackbird wings. **Morning Glories:** Cut seven 3½" circles from piece O. Hold each circle in the center and dip edges in Royal Blue dye bath. Dip the red morning glory (bottom right) in fuchsia. **Rock (lower right):** Dye 6 scrap pieces any colors you wish to form rock. They're cut like stripes to form a rainbow with the outside measuring 12½" wide by 6½" high.

TO ASSEMBLE QUILT: Stitch seams with ½" seam allowance using matching thread when possible. Press all dyed and dried pieces on the wrong side. **Cut border strips:** From grey piece (D) cut four 3½" × 86" and two 3½" × 71" lengths. From blue piece (C) cut two 3½" × 91" and two 3½" × 77". **Pink Sky (A):** Machine stitch velvet to batting piece 90" × 40". Make horizontal rows with straight stitches varying from 2"–7" wide the entire length of piece. Divide in half to get two pieces 19" × 90". Measure and trim to 86" long. **Central Panel (B,E,F,G) (plus gray strips (D)):** Sew stripes together varying colors and widths. Experiment to get a pleasing arrangement. Add a few silver

lamé slivers and some smaller stripes on top of wider ones—keep playing with them until you are happy. Cut a 28" circle to form "planet." Cut silver lamé ring 1½" wide and 29" in diameter. Cut gray outer ring 7" wide —38" in diameter. Stitch both rings to planet. Center blue sky pieces and planet onto batting 34" × 86". Pin in place. Stitch planet through batting using a zigzag stitch around edge of gray rings. Make rays with a straight stitch emanating from planet rim to edges of blue sky. Add 2 gray strips (D) along each side of central panel. **Appliqués:** Make paper patterns for clouds, birds and leaves. See color photo as a guide for placement and for cutting many of the freehand shapes. You will need to cut: 28 heart-shaped leaves 1½" × 2" from dark green piece (M), one large free-hand leaf approximately 14" long and 5½" wide at widest point also from M; 4 heart-shaped leaves 6" × 12" and 4 blue stems which are ½" freehand curves varying from 10"–20" from blue piece (I); about 20 pieces of long leafy marsh grass ranging from ½"–2" wide by 12"–41" long from green pieces (K & L); 5 freehand cloud shapes from white (P). When cutting birds, reverse pattern to match direction in photo. Use paper patterns to cut duplicate shapes of all pieces in fusible interfacing. Fuse interfacing to wrong side of velvet and trim appliqué so both edges are equal. This stabilizes velvet edges and makes it

easy to sew. (Otherwise . . . you'll have a terrible problem with wiggley edges!) Stitch each appliqué with a zigzag stitch or by hand with tiny overcast stitches. In some places you may have to sew by hand such as leaves that overlap from one section into another. Always apply smaller pieces to larger ones before attaching the quilt. Pad bird's breasts slightly as you sew to the bird. Clouds: Use a straight stitch to fill in curved areas to create a swirling effect. **Joining sections:** Stitch 3 main sections together. Stitch on outer gray (D) border and then blue border (C) both without any batting. **Quilt Back:** Piece together panels so that back is same size as front. To join back to front and add extra layer of batting: Spread out quilt front, face up. Place quilt back over it with right sides together. Spread a roll of polyester batting over wrong side and pin or baste the entire "sandwich" along edges. Leave an 18" opening for turning. Machine stitch, turn right side out. Slip stitch opening closed. **To tie quilt:** Thread a needle with 6-strand embroidery floss in matching or contrast thread. Take a single stitch from top going through all layers and back. Hand knot on top, leaving ends from ½" to 1" depending upon how you like the effect. Our designer used orange at the top of each border leaf, gray around planet perimeter and yellow for flower centers. Do as much as needed to keep batting from shifting.

PAINTED PILLOW DESIGNS

Read directions through carefully before starting.

MATERIALS: For each pillow you need: For painted design—cotton muslin (fine quality) 12″ × 12″. Scrap piece of cotton fabric for backing of quilting 12″ × 12″. Top frame around design—cotton velvet or velveteen 17″ × 17″ (your color choice). Pillow back—linen, linen-type fabric, or velvet to match top 17″ × 17″. Top padding—1 package polyester fiber. One spool each sewing thread—black, white, and color to match velvet. Pillow form—Kapok filling or standard pillow form 16″ × 16″. Coated paper plates. Straight pins. Compass. Paper towels. Paints—Flo-Paque Paints (available at arts and crafts stores). One bottle each will finish all four pillows:F40 Green; F30 Orange; F50 Dark Blue; F64 Maroon; F60 Purple; F71 Brown; F41 Leaf Green; F31 Yellow; F20 Red. One bottle Flo-Paque Dio-Sol (thinner). One small water color brush. One medium water color brush.

GENERAL INSTRUCTIONS for all pillows: Following directions on page 8, enlarge each design diagram. Prewash cotton muslin and iron flat. Cut a 12″ square. Transfer the design to the right side of this fabric using dressmakers carbon paper and tracing wheel. Draw a circle using a compass set on 5¾″ radius on both sides of the piece of scrap cotton fabric. Spread polyester fiber as evenly as possible within this circle. Lay the muslin with pattern over circle of stuffing and pin in place. Machine stitch through all thicknesses around circle with black thread. Relase pressure of pressure foot and stitch over all the line of pattern—use black thread and stitch through all thicknesses. To begin and end: stitch in the same place; this will secure the thread.

TO PAINT WITH FLO-PAQUE COLORS: Mix colors very well. If necessary, pour some of each onto a coated paper plate. These plates can be used again when the color has dried. Try out the color on a small piece of scrap muslin; try various brush strokes until you get a pleasing effect. Use paper towels to absorb excess liquid in areas where you do not want the color to spread. Quick strokes with the brush will reduce spreading; holding the brush in place on the fabric will cause the color to spread.

CHRYSANTHEMUM WITH BLUE AND MAROON BUTTERFLY: Colors needed: F40 Green—leaves and stems; F30 Orange—

flowers; F50 Dark Blue—wings of butterfly; F64 Maroon—back wings of butterfly; F60 Purple—outline of back wings; F71 Brown—outline of front wings. F1 Dio-Sol—Dilutant brush cleaner. Small water color brush. Medium water color brush. Work with each color separately, diluting it with Dio-Sol to get shade you want. Consistency should be that of water colors. Begin painting from center of each area so color will not spread out of stitched lines. For small areas, use dryer brush—after dipping in paint, touch to paper towel to absorb excess liquid. This keeps it from spreading.

IRIS WITH YELLOW AND PINK BUTTERFLY: Colors needed: F41 Leaf Green and F31 Yellow—light green leaves and bud; F40 Green—stem of bud, 3 leaves at base; F20 Red—for pink on butterfly; F50 Dark Blue—design on butterfly wings; F64 Maroon—center of butterfly. Dilute small amount of Green and paint in bud and three leaves at base. Mix together small amounts of Leaf Green and Yellow and dilute with Dio-Sol. Paint in bud and larger bud at left. Add more Dio-Sol and paint in other leaves, using a pale color. Paint yellow center area of butterfly. Dilute Red to make pink and paint on outer area of front wings and back wings. Make three dots on each front wing. Use Maroon for butterfly body and two center dots of back wings. Dilute Dark Blue to make light blue and paint outer areas of yellow design on front butterfly wings and circle around dots on back wings.

FRUIT STILL LIFE: Colors needed: F71 Brown—cutting board; F20 Red—apples; F30 Orange and F31 Yellow—pear and melon; F41 Leaf Green and F40 Green—stems. Dilute Leaf Green mixed with some Yellow for inside of melon and paint on, starting from inner area towards outer edges of stitched area. Do not paint seeds yet. Using same yellow-green color, paint one side of the pear. Dilute this color with more Dio-Sol and add more Yellow. Paint seeds and skin of melon and other side of pear. Dilute Brown and paint cutting board. Use drier brush when working near edges of areas. Add more Brown for darker area of side of board. Apples: Dilute Red to form light color and fill in apples except for stems. Add more Red color to mixture and paint darker areas of apples, leaving center area of each lighter for the highlights. Dilute Orange, add a small amount of Red and paint some streaks on apples. With this color, dab

brush on paper towel until it is almost dry and brush small amount on light side of pear. Dilute Green with very small amount of Dio-Sol and, using a dry brush, paint in stems.

PEONY WITH GREEN AND YELLOW BUTTERFLY: Colors needed: F64 Maroon—flower; F40 Green—leaves, stem and bud; F31 Yellow—butterfly; F41 Leaf Green. Dilute Maroon with small amount of Dio-Sol and paint in center of flower and areas where petals curl over. Using a drier brush helps keep color from spreading. Dilute same color with more Dio-Sol and paint other petals, beginning brush strokes toward center of flower and letting color spread toward outer edge of petals. Use Green on leaves and stem, with drier brush. Paint Yellow pattern on butterfly wings, and using Leaf Green mixed with some Yellow, paint outer edges of wings and dots on yellow areas.

TO MAKE PILLOW FRONTS: Cotton Velvet or Velveteen. Colors used: Green (Iris Pillow); Yellow Gold (Peony); Brown (Fruit Still Life);Rust (Chrysanthemum). Select a coordinated color of cotton fabric for facing circular cut-out. **For 16″ × 16″ Pillow:** Cut a square of velvet 17″ × 17″. Cut a square of cotton fabric 12″ × 12″. On wrong side of cotton, using a compass (set on 5½″), draw a circle. Mark center of this circle where point of compass rested. Place this on velvet square so that right sides are together and circle is facing you. Center circle by measuring from center mark on cotton so that it is 8½″ from all four sides. Pin in place and stitch around circle. Cut out inside of circle ¼″ from stitching and slash toward stitching every inch. Pull facing through center of circle and iron flat. Lay velvet, face up, over painted and padded muslin and pin in place. Stitch around circle ¼″ from inner edge.

TO MAKE PILLOW BACKS: Beige cotton linen-type fabric. Cut 17″ × 17″ square of fabric. Place on velvet front, right sides together, and pin in place. With a ruler, on backing side, draw lines ½″ from edges. If rounded corners are desired, use a glass and draw curves at corners. Sew around lines and curves, leaving one side unsewn, but sewing corners. Insert pillow form (we used Kapok filling). Hand stitch open side. These pillows can be dry cleaned as is, or covers can be removed by opening hand-stitched side.

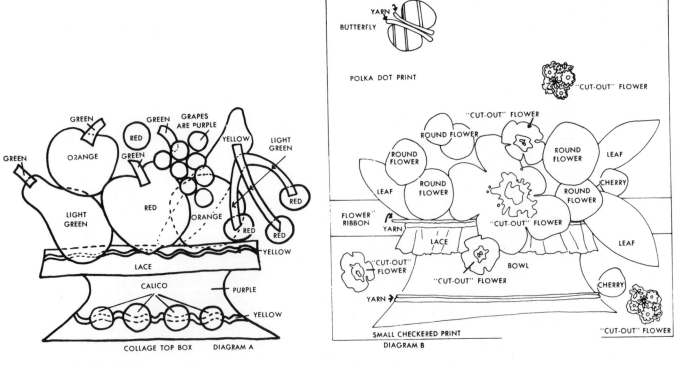

Diagram A labels: GREEN, GREEN, GRAPES ARE PURPLE, RED, GREEN, YELLOW, LIGHT GREEN, GREEN, ORANGE, GREEN, LIGHT GREEN, RED, ORANGE, RED, RED, RED, YELLOW, LACE, CALICO, PURPLE, YELLOW

COLLAGE TOP BOX   DIAGRAM A

Diagram B labels: YARN, BUTTERFLY, POLKA DOT PRINT, "CUT-OUT" FLOWER, "CUT-OUT" FLOWER, ROUND FLOWER, ROUND FLOWER, ROUND FLOWER, LEAF, LEAF, ROUND FLOWER, ROUND FLOWER, CHERRY, LEAF, FLOWER RIBBON, YARN, "CUT-OUT" FLOWER, LACE, LEAF, "CUT-OUT" FLOWER, BOWL, "CUT-OUT" FLOWER, "CUT-OUT" FLOWER, YARN, CHERRY, SMALL CHECKERED PRINT, "CUT-OUT" FLOWER

DIAGRAM B

COLLAGE TOP BOX

MATERIALS: One wooden box 4″ × 8″ × 4½″. (Variation: cigar box, shoe box, metal file box.) Bright yellow striped calico print for outside of box, green felt to cover bottom of box, red calico for lining (and to include in collage decoration). White household glue. Scissors. Brush for applying glue. Felt (2″ sqs) 1 color each of red, orange, yellow, two shades green, purple. Small amount of yellow rick rack. Small piece of lace approximately 3″ long.

TO MAKE: Measure and cut out yellow material according to size of box. Apply a thin coat of glue to backside of fabric, being sure to smooth out cloth as you work. Cover lower portion of box with a single piece of yellow fabric (stripes running horizontally). Overlap fabric ½″ on bottom of box, mitering corners. Bring fabric over top edge and down into box ½″. Cover two ends of box top (vertical stripes) in like manner. Cover curved top with single piece of fabric. Line with red calico. Apply felt to bottom. To make collage fruit bowl decoration, enlarge Diagram A, following directions on page 8. Cut out decorative pieces. Arrange on box top first to make sure you have proper effect. Remove and paste down piece by piece, following Diagram A and photo.

COLLAGE PICTURE

MATERIALS: 2 pieces of illustration board, size to be determined by the size of your collage (ours measured 17″ × 17″ for the background and 11″ × 11″ for the collage). Checkered material to cover background. An alternate checkered pattern for base of picture. Piece of polka dot fabric for top of picture. Scraps of lace. Ribbon. Yarn. Piece of floral material from which to cut out flowers. Calico print for bowl. An alternate color calico print for round-shaped flowers. Green material (print or plain) for leaves. Scrap of red felt for cherries. Scrap of plaid or stripe for butterfly. White household glue. Brush for applying glue. Sharp scissors.

TO MAKE: Using Diagram B enlarge to desired size, following instructions on page 8. Following Diagram B and photo, cut out materials into approximate sizes and colors shown. Apply a thin coat of glue to backside of fabric and being sure to smooth out cloth as you work, paste down checkered base, polka dot background and ribbon allowing about ½″ extra all sides to turn and paste to back of illustration board. Be sure that all checkered areas are laid out evenly by placing first row of checkers along top edge of work, smoothing out along the way. Before pasting down any part of the flower bowl collage, arrange pieces on the background to make sure you are pleased with the effect; then remove and build up collage, adding yarn, lace and ribbon decorations. Cover background matte with checkered fabric, turning about ½″ fabric to back of illustration board. Center collage to matte; paste; frame if desired.

RICKRACK STRIPED BOX

MATERIALS: One unfinished wooden box 11½″ × 8″ × 8½″. (Variation: cigar box, shoe box, metal file box.) Strips of calico material (or any small floral print, gingham, etc.), preferably red, yellow, blue and green cut to 2″ widths. Two packages of blue rick rack. White household glue. Brush to apply glue. Scissors. Enough felt to cover bottom of box.

TO MAKE: Cut out, in varying colors, the 2″ wide strips (or stripes in proportion to the measurement of the box used). Be sure to cut the strips 1″ longer in length for overlapping. Select your arrangement of colors for top and sides. Apply a thin coat of glue to backside of the strip and apply vertically (overlapping about ½″ each onto the bottom and down into the box), being sure to smooth out cloth as you work. Continue to apply strips in same fashion until you have covered the entire outer box (minus bottom). Line the inside of box and top with one calico print only. (We used red.) Trim between strip with rick rack, covering each seam. Apply felt to bottom. **NOTE:** Be sure to trim material away from hinges so that top of box will lay flat.

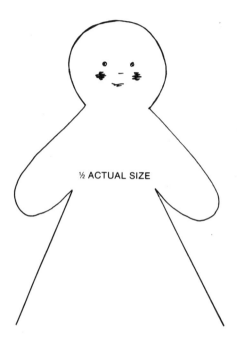

½ ACTUAL SIZE

SHADOW BOX

MATERIALS: Shadow box—available at American Handicrafts stores nationwide—9½″ × 12½″ × 1¾″. Wood stain in color of choice. Print fabric for frame background —9½″ × 12½″. Spray adhesive. Laces: a variety of lace in ecru and white: ¾ yd of 1″ flat lace; ¾ yd of ½″ wide floral motif lace; ⅛ yd of 3″ wide ruffled lace for apron; ⅛ yd of 1¼″ wide lace for basket; ¼ yd of ¾″ ruffled eyelet for petticoat and inside of basket; ½ yd of ⅛″ lace trim for swing and basket handle; lace doily. Natural muslin: ¼ yd Polyester fiberfill: a few handfuls. Pearl cotton: small amounts of white (or white string). Print fabric for doll underskirt—4″ × 10″. Solid fabric for skirt: 4″ × 10″. Yarn Scraps: 2-ply, 2 shades of brown. Embroidery floss or thread: small amounts of blue, peach and red. Tapestry needle.

TO MAKE DOLL: Cut 2 dolls shapes from pattern A. **Face:** Embroider on front as shown. Blue French knots for eyes. Peach satin stitch for cheeks. A single peach stitch for nose. 3 freehand red stitches for mouth. Stitch doll right sides together, leave lower edge open. Clip curves and turn. Turn up ¼″ hem with a hand running stitch. Stuff lightly with polyester fiberfill. Sew closed. **Hair:** Use a tapestry needle to insert strands of yarn through seam at top of head. Glue strands at side of doll's face. Braid into pigtail. **Cap:** Use small lace motif clipped from center of doily. Within the large circle, make a small circle of running stitches. Gather to fit doll's head. Sew in place. Turn up brim in front and stitch it in place. Use lace doily to make shawl. **Underskirt:** stitch side seams; fold print fabric lengthwise. Make machine or hand gathers. **Skirt:** stitch side seams; fold solid fabric lengthwise. Make machine or hand gathers. Hand tack about 10″ of ruffled eyelet to inside of finished doll's skirt so that it peeks out between hem and print ruffle underskirt. Sew skirts in place. **Apron:** use a piece of 3″ wide ruffled lace, fasten or slip stitch at waist.

TO MAKE SHADOWBOX: Remove cardboard backing of shadow box. Stain wood. Arrange lace pieces on background fabric (see photo) using a variety of lace pieces. Glue or zigzag stitch pieces into pleasing position. Use spray adhesive to apply fabric to the cardboard backing following instructions on can. Replace cardboard with lace and fabric background into shadow box. **Doll Basket:** Use a 6″ strip of 1¼″ flat lace trim for outside of basket. Slip stitch ends and lower edges, planning to have seam in back. Line basket with several layers of ruffled lace, lightly stuff with fiberfill and a 6″ long folded strip of floral lace motifs. Tack to basket edges, planning some motifs spilling over top. Use 7″ of the narrowest lacy trim for basket handle. Slip stitch or glue onto basket. Position and glue basket in the lower right corner of shadow box. (See photo.) **Doll Swing:** Use 20″ of narrow lacy trim to make swing. Place doll in center of lace; tack hands and back as needed. Attach swinging doll to top of box with tiny stitches within lacy framework.

CACHE

MATERIALS: Sturdy cardboard gift box (ours is 7″ × 8″ × 3″). Fabric: Amount to cover box lid plus allowance for turning under (ours is 16″ × 17½″). One antique doily. Spray adhesive.

TO MAKE: Cut fabric to fit lid plus sides and 1″ to 2″ allowance for turning under. Use spray adhesive to apply fabric to box lid following instructions on can. Apply fabric to lid as if you were wrapping a package. Do whatever is comfortable as long as all fabric is flat and adheres to lid. You may need to trim bulk at corners or under folds at two ends. Spray back of doily with spray adhesive and center it on the lid.

GENERAL INSTRUCTIONS FOR MACHINE EMBROIDERY: Machine embroidery is fast, it's easy, and it's true that anyone can do it even if they've never sewn before. Or, if you do sew but have trouble keeping a straight line, this may be just the needlecraft you've been waiting for. Machine stitchery is really just decorative darning, or darning turned art. The key to success is practice and experimentation. Your free-floating stitches become like brush strokes, and it helps to think of the needle as a paintbrush. You'll have to test your technique with each fabric. At first you'll feel all thumbs—and then suddenly you'll get the hang of it and things will speed along. The faster you go, the easier and smoother it becomes; and the more you practice, the faster you'll go. The speed factor is what makes it so appealing—you can closely duplicate hand embroidery with finished results in one third to one half the time.

MATERIALS: Any sewing machine. A zigzag feature is a bonus. Machine embroidery thread in size = 50 or = 30 in assorted colors. Size = 50 is finer, and better for lighter fabrics. Use = 30 for heavier fabrics to give a bold effect. There's a wide variety of this special thread now available in most fabric stores, notion counters and through sewing machine dealers. Pick up different types and decide which ones work best for you. Some have a glossy appearance, and others are flat but come in brilliant colors. Background fabric 14″ × 18″ (includes 2″ margin—actual panel is 12″ × 16″)—the heavier the better and more for sample. Border fabric and background fabric: ½ yd. An assortment of fabric scraps in different colors, shapes, textures—solids and prints. Clear plastic presser foot—makes it easy to see what you're doing. Wooden dowel: ½″ × 17½″. Staple gun and wooden board for blocking. Tissue paper or regular notebook paper. Sometimes this is helpful when placed underneath your work as it prevents puckers. After stitching is completed, simply tear paper away. Size 11 sewing machine needle. Handy items such as a small screwdriver, tweezers, a seam ripper, small embroidery or round-tipped scissors.

FOR YOUR PRACTICE SESSION: First check your machine to be sure that it's clean and properly working. Lint buildup contributes to thread breakage, and you'll have to check and brush it frequently to keep it clean. Lower the feed dog, or cover it according to your sewing machine manual. This is not absolutely crucial and will depend on the results you get through experimenting. Cut 14″ × 18″ piece and set aside. Cut a sample piece. Draw, trace or transfer a simple motif on the right side of your sample piece. Lower the presser foot. This is very important and is easy to forget. If you do forget, the thread will get all tangled up in the bobbin area. Pull up bobbin thread and hold while you make a few stitches. Cut off threads before stitching over. Your arms should be resting on the table. Use your hands to guide the hoop. Forefingers can be placed near the stitching area to keep fabric from popping up or skipping stitches. BE CAREFUL! Place little fingers and thumbs

around the ring as shown. Stitch in a jogging motion. Slide the hoop back and forth very gently while stitching as fast as you comfortably can. This step needs practice. Once you've practiced and feel comfortable with machine embroidery, you're ready to begin your stitchery and appliqué hanging.

APPLIQUÉ HANGING

This is an easy machine stitchery project because anything you do will look terrific. You really can't go wrong. The more you do, the better it will look. If you're not happy with one part, just cover with fabric and more stitching.

SIZE SHOWN: 16½″ × 20½″.

TO MAKE: Following directions on page 8, enlarge design diagram. Transfer the design to the right side of your fabric using dressmaker's carbon paper and tracing wheel. Cut shapes and arrange on background fabric. Pin. Baste. Set sewing machine on darn. (Leave tension in normal position.) Do an all-over stitching to secure pieces. Stitch details working from the center out. This helps avoid puckering, though don't worry when some puckering happens. (You'll block it later.) Do as much as you can with one color thread at a time. Keep the bobbin thread color close to the top thread color. Try to do one all-over layer of stitching before going

back into an area for detail work. This helps cut down on puckering . . . and the possibility of the thread breaking. However, don't panic if the thread breaks—it happens. Check the machine often for lint build-up. Frequent cleanings help prevent thread from breaking. Go back over initial stitching and stitch details with a contrast thread color. Make smaller clusters of circles, pointed flower shapes and loops outlined several times as shown in photo and on graph. Do a final cross-grid stitching going back and forth over previous stitching in another color to give additional detail and texture to your stitchery painting. **Blocking:** Staple stitchery to heavy wood board placing staples very close together. First, make a row of staples along the top. Then, pull piece taut and staple lower edge. Repeat for sides, making it as tight as possible. Take a clean, damp sponge and soak the entire piece with water. Let dry. The piece should be quite flat. Pry up staples and remove stitchery. Trim off excess allowance, leaving ½″ seam allowance to join border fabric. Cut 3½″ strips of border fabric and join with a ½″ seam allowance to stitchery. Cut a piece of backing fabric the same size as the finished stitchery with border and stitch with right sides together leaving a 3″ opening. Trim and clip corners. Turn. Press. Slip stitch opening closed. Whipstitch dowel to the top of the stitchery at inch and a half intervals.

1/3 ACTUAL SIZE

SEWING MACHINE PORTRAITS

Give friends or relatives a personal present: a portrait of their house or family.

MATERIALS: A favorite snapshot of house or family. Fabric scraps. Iron-on fusible backing. Zigzag sewing machine. Paper on which to enlarge portrait. Tracing paper for patterns. Thread.

TO MAKE: Enlarge snapshot following directions on page 8 or have photo professionally enlarged. Trace your enlarged picture for appliqué shapes. Keep in mind special details: the family pet, hair styles, even the knocker on the door. Cut out appliqué shapes and use as pattern pieces. Select fabrics with your picture in mind: blue for the sky, a variety of green prints for trees and shrubs, gingham for a rooftop. Think of small calicos for dresses, bits of lace for necklines and plain colors for skin tones and men's clothes. Cut out appliqué shapes and place on a suitable background fabric. Secure with iron-on fusible backing or basting. (If you baste, machine straight stitch close to the raw edges.) Outline pieces with a satin stitch on the sewing machine. Embroider any small details by hand. Frame your art or finish it as a pillow.

SEWING MACHINE LANDSCAPES

Illustrations from a child's book can be transformed into wall hangings using simple appliqué techniques.

SIZE: 27″ × 51″ finished.

MATERIALS: Child's picture book for inspiration. Brown wrapping paper. Tracing paper. Fabric scraps. Unbleached muslin 29″ × 53″. Iron-on fusible backing. Thread. Piece of ⅜″ thick fiber board 27″ × 51″ or wide bias tape and wooden dowel 55″ long or longer. Wire or cup hooks for hanging.

TO MAKE: Take a child's picture book and copy or adapt elements from one or several illustrations. Following directions on page 8, enlarge your design (or sketch your ideas on a piece of brown wrapping paper that is the same size as the finished wall hanging will be.) Trace your enlarged design for appliqué shapes. Select fabrics with your picture in mind: use simulated fur for animals, corduroy to suggest the wood of a barn, leather-like vinyl for a hippo, green-printed fabrics for the leaves of trees, black satin for sea lions, pink satin for mother pig and her piglets, etc. Let your imagination roam freely through your collection of scraps to find the most amusing and whimsical fabric for each element of the composition. Cut out appliqué shapes: first the larger background areas, then the smaller areas, animals and people. Start with a piece of unbleached muslin slightly larger than the desired finished size, and secure the background pieces to the muslin with iron-on fusible backing or basting. (If you baste, machine straight stitch close to the raw edges.) Outline pieces with a zig-zag satin stitch on the sewing machine. After the background is sewn, add the smaller appliqués; if these pieces are very small, sew them on by hand using a slipstitch. Add accents such as hair, eyes or flowers with hand embroidery. To display, you can wrap the completed wall hanging around a piece of ⅜″ thick fiber board or stitch a piece of wide bias tape by hand to the wrong side of the piece and insert a wooden dowel. Hang with wire or cup hooks.

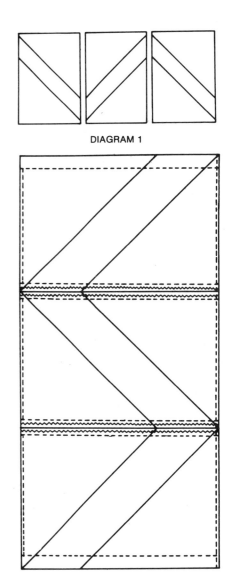

DIAGRAM 1

CABANA

SIZE: 5' high and 11¼' long.

MATERIALS: Sturdy cotton twill 46" wide: green, 7½ yds; blue, 6 yds; orange, 1⅓ yds; and yellow, ¾ yds. One package of bias seam tape in orange and in yellow. Thread to match fabric colors. Four wooden dowels 6' long and ¾" in diameter.

TO MAKE: From the blue, cut three panels 62" long and the width of the fabric, and two pocket strips 13½" × 38¼". From the green, cut three panels 62" long and the width of the fabric; then cut three lengthwise strips 12" wide and 76" long. From the yellow, cut two pocket strips 13¼" × 38¼". From the orange, cut one piece 23¼" × 42¼" and another piece 23¼" × 27¼". Fold the yellow and the blue pocket strips in half with right sides facing to measure 6⅝" × 38¼". Match edges and stitch leaving an opening to turn. Turn to right side and press. Slipstitch opening closed. On two of the green panels, position a yellow and a blue pocket on the right side as shown in the

photograph. Topstitch short ends to panels. Form pocket sections by topstitching strips of orange bias tape over pockets as shown in the photograph. Topstitch along bottom of some of the sections to close pockets. Leave some open if you wish. Make a narrow hem along one short edge of the small orange section. Place this section over one end of the large section, right sides facing and edges even. The double layer forms the pocket and the single layer is the flap. Stitch the two sections together. Clip corners. Turn to the right side and press. Hem the raw edges of the flap by turning them ¼", then ⅜" and stitching. Decorate the flap by topstitching yellow bias tape around the edge as shown in the photograph. Place pocket on the right side of the third green panel as shown in the photograph and topstitch in place. With right sides facing, stitch the three green panels together to form one long panel. Press seams open. Set machine for a wide zigzag. On right side, zigzag about ¼" from seamline to keep seam allowances flat. Press the long edges of the green strips ½" to the wrong sides. Pin to the right side

of the blue panels positioning as shown in Diagram 1. Top and bottom of each strip should be 1" from top and bottom of panel edge. Topstitch strips to panels along edges. Trim strip edges even with edges of panels. Stitch panels together to form one long panel as shown in Diagram 2. Press seams open and zigzag as done with green panel. Press the top and bottom edges of both panels 1" to the wrong side. Place these two panels with right sides facing. Pin and stitch short ends. Turn to right side and press. Match the top edges and pin. Topstitch close to edge from end to end. Pin along the vertical seams through both fabric layers. Seams of the green and the blue should be lying on top of one another. Now stitch the casings that will hold the tent poles. Stitch 2" from each end and 1" on each side of the vertical seams to form four casings. See Diagram 2. Pin the bottom edges together and topstitch. Do not stitch across casing openings. Insert the poles in the casings. Set up the cabana, working the poles into the sand. Stash your beach belongings in the pockets and enjoy your day in the sun.

PORTABLE PAVILION

CANOPY

SIZE: 11′ × 46″

MATERIALS: 7½ yds of heavy striped fabric, 48″ wide. 4 aluminum poles (2 packages of Sears Roebuck #6A-78613C). 6 1″ metal rings. 30 ft of twine to anchor the 4 poles. 6 tent skewers.

TO MAKE: With right sides facing, fold fabric in half widthwise. Stitch each long edge in a 1″ seam. Turn to right side and press. At the end, turn the raw edges to the inside 3″ and topstitch them together. To form the canopy, measure and mark along both long edges 12″ and 60″ from the fold end. Attach metal rings at these distances and at each corner of the topstitched end. Rings should extend beyond fabric's edge. Use a strong thread and sew rings securely. Set up your canopy placing the poles through the rings and planting them in the sand as shown in the photograph. Tie twine to top of each pole, pull it taut and anchor it in the sand with tent skewers. Put skewers through the rings at the back end and anchor in sand.

TERRY CLOTH MAT

SIZE: 83″ × 45″

MATERIALS: 4⅔ yds of terry cloth, 45–46″ wide. 2⅔ yds of the same fabric used for the canopy.

TO MAKE: Fold the terry cloth length in half, wrong sides together, to get a rectangle 7 ft long. Staystitch edges to hold the double thickness. Using the photograph as a color guide, cut strips of fabric 9½″ wide to get two panels 84″ long and two 46″ long. Form a rectangle with panels, matching stripes and mitering corners. Place striped rectangle with its right side facing terry, matching corners and edges. Stitch around outer edge in a 1″ seam. Trim corners, turn to right side and press. Turn the inner edge ½″ to the wrong side. Pin and topstitch to terry.

BOLSTERS

SIZE: each is 8″ in diameter and 23″ long.

MATERIALS: 1 yd of the same fabric used for the canopy. 2 22″ zippers. 2 foam rubber bolsters in the size given above.

TO MAKE: Fold fabric in half lengthwise. For each bolster, cut a piece 24″ × 27″, and 2 circles 9″ in diameter. Baste 24″ edges together in a ⅝″ seam, forming a tube, Press seam open. Insert zipper by hand. Staystitch ½″ form each end of tube. Clip to staystitching at ¾″ intervals. With right sides facing, pin a circle to each end. Stitch just beyond staystitching. Turn cover to right side and insert bolster.

Choose a heavy fabric that does not ravel such as sailcloth, duck, canvas or a sturdy furnishing fabric. Some fabrics will need to be backed for the bag to hold its shape. **NOTE:** All seam allowances are ½" unless indicated otherwise.

TOTE BAGS 1, 2, 4, 7, 8 and 9

GENERAL INSTRUCTIONS: To make your bag, read the following. Then read the individual instructions before cutting the pattern. For bags 8 and 9, go directly to the individual instructions. Following Diagram 1, cut a paper pattern adjusting dimensions for the bag you are making. Cut pattern twice in the fabric. Place fabric sections, right sides facing, and stitch bottom seam E. Press seam open. Press seam edges under ¼" and stitch to bag on each side of seam to strengthen. With right sides facing, stitch side seams B. Press and finish like the bottom seam. To hem top edge, press ½" to wrong side. Now, press this edge under 2" and stitch. Following Diagram 2, stitch bottom side seams. Turn to right side. Press sharp creases on each side edge and two bottom edges. Topstitch ⅛" from each crease to make it permanent. See Diagram 3. Cut, sew and attach handles following instructions for the bag you are making. Cut cardboard to fit the bag bottom. Cut a slightly larger piece of fabric and glue it to cardboard turning under edges. Place in bottom of bag to stiffen.

BAG No. 2—The right size for all your shopping.

SIZE: 14" high, 17" wide with side and base 5" wide.

MATERIALS: 1¼ yd of 44–45" fabric.

TO MAKE: Following Diagram 1, cut pattern to measure: A 24", B 17", C 3", D 3" and E 18". For handles, cut two strips 18" × 4". Fold and stitch as for Bag No. 1. Attach to outside as shown in photograph.

BAG No. 1—Perfect for carrying long loaves or a bottle of wine.

SIZE: 18" high, 13" wide with side and base 4" wide.

MATERIALS: ¾ yd of 44–45" fabric.

TO MAKE: Following Diagram 1, cut pattern to measure: A 19", B 21", C 2½", D 2½", E 14". For handles, cut two strips 14" × 3". Press all edges of strip ½" to wrong side. Now, press strip in half lengthwise. Topstitch all around edges. Position handles as shown in photograph lapping ends 2½" to inside. Stitch in a rectangle and then a cross as shown in Diagram 3. To divide bag into sections, stitch a double row down the middle starting 2" from top and ending 2" from bottom. Omit cardboard.

BAG No. 4—A large tote for weekend travel.

SIZE: 20" high, 20" wide with side and base 7" wide.

MATERIALS: 1¾ yds of 44–45" fabric.

TO MAKE: Following diagram 1, cut pattern to measure: A 29", B 23", C 4", D 4" and E 21". For handles, cut strips 14" × 4". Fold, stitch and attach to inside as for Bag No. 1 adjusting to a comfortable length for you.

BAG No. 7—Holds all the working girl's gear.

SIZE: 16" high, 14" wide with side and base 5" wide.

MATERIALS: 1 yd of 44–45" fabric.

TO MAKE: Following diagram 1, cut pattern to measure: A 21", B 19", C 3", D 3" and E 15". See Bag No. 1 for cutting and making handles.

BAGS Nos. 8 and 9—For mother and daughter.

SIZES: 12" × 12" and 6" × 6".

MATERIALS: ½ yd of 44–45" fabric.

TO MAKE: For the large bag, cut a piece of fabric 28" × 13" and two handles 18" × 3". For the child's bag, cut a piece 14" × 7" and two handles 10" × 2". To hem each short end of bag, press edge ¼" to wrong side. Press again 1¾" and stitch. With right sides facing, fold bag in half matching hem edges. Pin and stitch side seams. Turn to right side. Fold, stitch and attach handles as for Bag No. 1. The small bag is made like the large one, turning a 1" hem.

SHOULDER BAG

SIZE: 6" high, 6" wide with a gusset 2½" wide.

MATERIALS: ⅔ yd of 44–45" fabric, a lining scrap for flap, and a double buckle with a prong to fit a strap 2½" wide.

TO MAKE: Following Diagrams 4 and 5, draw paper patterns. Cut one bag section for each pattern. From Diagram 4, cut lining for flap up to overlay line. Press straight edges of lining ½" to wrong side. With right sides facing, stitch lining to bag flap around curved edge from A to B. Clip to stitching at A and B. Notch curved edge. Turn to right side and press. Topstitch curved edge and overlay edge. On bag front, fold straight edge 1" to wrong side and stitch. To make strap, cut 4" wide strips and join to get 152". Strip will form a continuous gusset-shoulder strap. Fold in half on the width to get a strip 76" long. Press all lengthwise edges ¾" to wrong side. Slip buckle on one thickness of strip and slide to fold end. Make a little hole and push prong through fabric. See Diagram 6. Starting 8" from buckle, place the raw edge of the bag front between folded edges of strip ½" and pin. Match remainder of folded edges on this side of strap and pin. See Diagram 7. Starting at buckle on right side of bag, stitch close to edges around bag to end of strip. Place the raw edge of the bag back between the folded edges of the strap in the same way and baste. Turn inside out. Stitch on right side. Fold strap end to wrong side to form a point and stitch. To close flap, place a gripper snap at the X marks in Diagrams 4 and 5. Make a row of eyelets on the strap for buckling and adjusting.

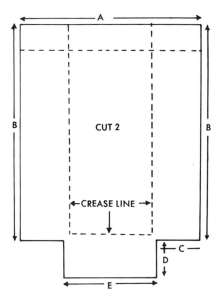

DIAGRAM 1

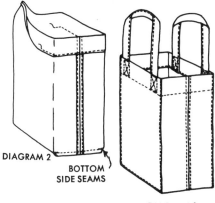

DIAGRAM 2

BOTTOM SIDE SEAMS

DIAGRAM 3

TOTE BAGS

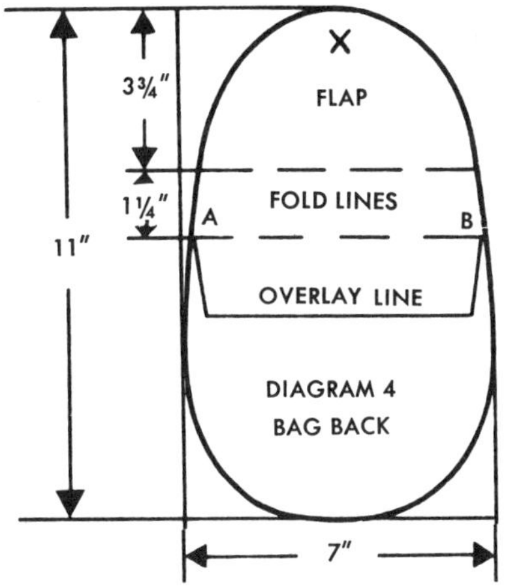

3¾"

1¼"

11"

X

FLAP

A   FOLD LINES   B

OVERLAY LINE

DIAGRAM 4
BAG BACK

7"

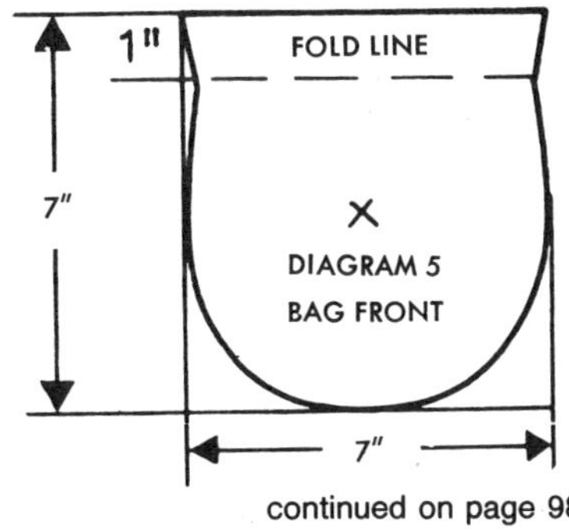

1"

FOLD LINE

7"

X

DIAGRAM 5
BAG FRONT

7"

continued on page 98

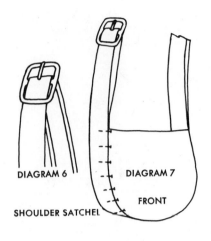

DIAGRAM 6

DIAGRAM 7
FRONT

SHOULDER SATCHEL

DOLL CARRIER

SIZE: 19″ long, 7½″ wide and about 14″ high.

MATERIALS: 1¼ yd of 44–45″ fabric. Cardboard. Split paper fasteners.

TO MAKE: Following Diagram 8, cut the carrier once. Following directions on page 8, enlarge Diagram 9 on paper for the hood. Place this pattern on fold of fabric and cut once. For handles, cut two strips 40″ × 3″. Join strip ends to form a circle. Then press raw edges ½″ to wrong side and fold to get a 1″ width. Topstitch close to both edges. Pin and topstitch to sides and base of bag as shown in Diagram 8. With right sides facing, pin and stitch the 7″ seams at each corner to form a box shape. Press top edge ¼″ to wrong side. Then, press it ¾″ to wrong side and stitch along both edges. To stiffen corners, cut pieces of cardboard 6″ × 2″. Fold in half lengthwise. Cover with fabric cut ½″ larger. Glue, turning under edges. Glue cardboard in each corner. Stiffen base with a cardboard rectangle, covered with fabric and glued in the same way. To make hood, match edges of each dart. Pin and stitch. Trim seam close to stitching. Press hood front 2″ to wrong side. Insert a cardboard strip to stiffen. Stitch close to raw edge and folded edge. Finish bottom edge with a narrow hem. Attach hood to carrier at sides with paper fasteners where shown in photograph.

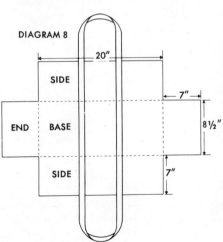

DIAGRAM 8

20″

SIDE

7″

END · BASE

8½″

SIDE

7″

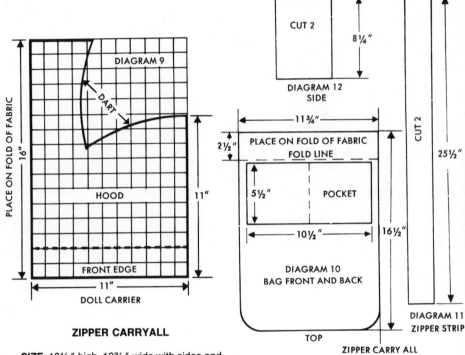

DIAGRAM 9

PLACE ON FOLD OF FABRIC

16″

DART

HOOD

11″

FRONT EDGE

11″

DOLL CARRIER

ZIPPER CARRYALL

SIZE: 13½″ high, 10¾″ wide with sides and base 5″ wide.

MATERIALS: 1 yd of 44–45″ fabric. 24″ zipper.

TO MAKE: Following Diagrams 10, 11 and 12, make paper patterns including a pocket pattern. Fold fabric in half lengthwise. Pin bag front and back, and the long edge of the pocket on fabric's fold. Pin other pieces and cut. Transfer fold lines on front and back to right side of fabric with chalk pencil. For handles, cut two strips 20″ × 3″. Fold pocket in half with right sides facing. Stitch seams leaving an opening for turning. Clip corners and trim seams. Turn to right side. Press. Topstitch 1″ from fold edge. With fold edge facing top of bag, center pocket on right side with its bottom edge just above fold line. Topstitch to bag. Stitch down center to form two sections. At base of bag, clip seam allowance exactly ½″ on each fold line so fabric will spread to fit side gusset. Press one 6″ edge of each side gusset to wrong side. With right sides facing, pin side gusset to bottom and sides of bag. Turned edge should face bag's top. See Diagram 13. Stitch seam with bag side up. Press one long edge of each zipper strip ⅝″ to wrong side. Topstitch turned edges close to each side of zipper coil or teeth. With right sides facing, pin long edges of strip around bag sides and top. See Diagram 14. Clip strip at corner so it will spread to fit bag. Short ends of strip should be covered by side gusset. Stitch both seams. On outside, stitch close to turned edge of side gusset. Fold stitch and attach handles as for Bag No. 1, placing them where shown in photograph. Stiffen base with a cardboard rectangle as done with Tote Bags.

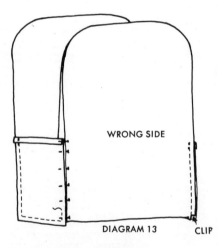

6″

CUT 2

8¼″

DIAGRAM 12
SIDE

3½″

11¾″

2½″ PLACE ON FOLD OF FABRIC
FOLD LINE

5½″   POCKET

10½″

16½″

DIAGRAM 10
BAG FRONT AND BACK

TOP

CUT 2

25½″

DIAGRAM 11
ZIPPER STRIP

ZIPPER CARRY ALL

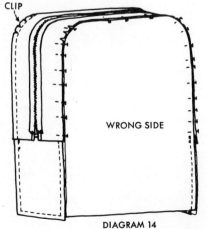

WRONG SIDE

DIAGRAM 13   CLIP

CLIP

WRONG SIDE

DIAGRAM 14

FOR CHILDREN

Make something that a child won't remember ever being without.

Here is a pied piper to lead someone to sunshine . . . a little girl's wardrobe right out of a fairy tale . . . a big soft walrus to snuggle against . . . and a quaint patchwork quilt. Here are stocking dolls with button eyes . . . and a doll with a yellow raincoat. A mola sun god to make you—and the recipient—proud . . . and a Russian family in embroidered finery.

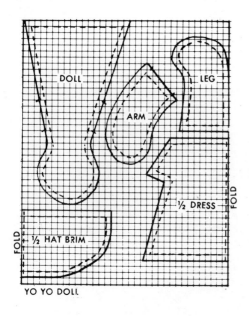

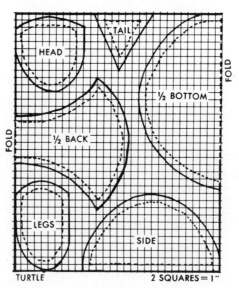

YO YO DOLL

TURTLE   2 SQUARES = 1"

YO YO LADY

MATERIALS: ½ yd light pink cotton for body. ¼ yd dark pink cotton for dress. Scraps of cotton prints for yo yos, bonnet and sash. Lace or eyelet for dress trim. Yarn for hair. Buttons for eyes, mouth, nose. Cotton batting.

TO MAKE: Doll: Enlarge pattern following directions on page 8. Cut 2 pink doll pieces, 4 pink arm pieces; 4 pink leg pieces. Stitch legs and arms; invert and stuff. Place arms between 2 doll pieces and stitch around, leaving lower edge of body open. Invert, press and stuff. Pin legs to lower edge and

stitch closed. Stitch on, in style desired, yarn hair and button features. **Dress:** Using pattern, cut 2 dress pieces; cut 5" slit for center back opening and stitch tiny hem around it. Stitch side and shoulder seams. For sleeves gather 2 strips 4½" × 17". Stitch to arm hole. Gather neck and cuffs and stitch on ruffled trim. Turn hem and stitch on trim. **Bonnet:** Cut 2 hat brim pieces, (facing piece a different color if desired). With right sides facing, stitch curved edge, clip seams; invert and press. For cap of bonnet cut strip 6" × 24". Hem the two 6" sides; gather one 24" edge and stitch it along straight side of brim. Gather other side of 24" strip and pull up

tightly so that bonnet fits properly. Tack together at base of gathering. **Sash:** Cut and stitch a piece 4" × 30" for bow at back of apron. **Apron:** Make about 34 yo yos as directed below. Arrange them on top of dress as desired, using single row straps. Join yo yos by placing 2 right sides together and tacking. Continue until all are joined. **Yo Yos:** Cut 4½" circles of lightweight cotton prints, using cardboard circle for a pattern. Turn in and pin ¼" hem allowance. With needle and thread make a running stitch on hem allowance, then pull up thread, gathering as tightly as possible. Flatten and press. The opening is on the top side of yo yo.

YO YO TURTLE

MATERIALS: ½ yd green cotton. ½ yd yellow print cotton. Cotton batting for stuffing. 2 buttons for eyes. Cotton print scraps for yo yos.

TO MAKE: Make 33 yo yos as directed below. Enlarge patterns for turtle following directions on page 8. Cut 8 legs, 2 heads, 2

tails, 1 bottom, 2 sides, 1 back. Stitch sides to back. Stitch legs, head and tail, invert, press and stuff. Pin in place between back and bottom. Stitch all around except for 3" under tail. Turn to right side and stuff. Stitch end closed. Pin yo yos on back and tack in place with tiny invisible stitches. Stitch on button eyes.

Yo Yos: Cut 4½" circles of lightweight cotton prints, using cardboard circle for a pattern. Turn in and pin ¼" hem allowance. With needle and thread make a running stitch on hem allowance, then pull up thread, gathering as tightly as possible. Flatten and press. The opening is on the top side of yo yo.

DISC PIPER

MATERIALS: Scraps of cotton prints. Batting for stuffing. Yarn for hair. Buttons for features. Ribbon for shoe trim. Yarn needle. String for joining discs.

TO MAKE: Cut 30 cotton circles in various prints and checks 6½" diameter, and 30 circles of batting the same size. Place 2 circles, right sides together with batting disc on top. Stitch all around except for 2" opening. Clip batting close to stitch line. Invert and press. Stitch opening closed. Continue thus to make 15 discs for the body. Using same pro-

cess, make 52 discs for arms and legs using a circle 4¾" diameter. Use 16 discs per leg, 10 discs per arm. Join with yarn or string stitched through centers and knotted at joints. Enlarge pattern pieces for head, hands and feet following directions on page 8. Cut 4 heads, 4 feet, 4 hands. Stitch, invert and stuff. Stitch on to doll. Wrap yarn for hair around piece of cardboard 8" long, then tie at top, cut at bottom. Stitch top to head. Repeat until hair is completed. Trim bangs. Stitch on button eyes and mouth, and bows on shoes.

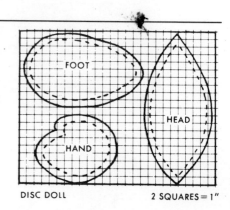

DISC DOLL   2 SQUARES = 1"

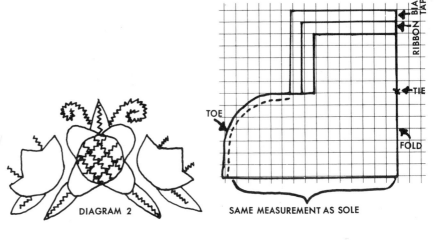

DIAGRAM 1   CENTER FRONT
SCALE: 1 SQ= ½"

DIAGRAM 2

DIAGRAM 3

RIBBON BIAS TAPE

TIE

FOLD

TOE

SAME MEASUREMENT AS SOLE

COLOR AND CUTTING KEY:
A. CUT 1—DRESS FABRIC D. CUT 1 — PINK
B. CUT 4 — WHITE   E. CUT 2 — PINK
C. CUT 2 — PINK   F. CUT 2 — WHITE

PATCHWORK COAT

MATERIALS: Coat pattern one size larger than usual. Patchwork fabric according to pattern. You may make patchwork of any fabric, but for cleaning purposes fabrics of compatible content should be used. Fur lining according to pattern. Fur trim. Braid trim for front and armhole edges.

TO MAKE: Sew together patches of various sizes until you have the same amount of fabric as pattern calls for. Cut and assemble coat according to pattern directions. Using the same pattern pieces as used for the outside of the coat, cut fronts, sleeves and back from lining fabric. Stitch lining to coat, leaving an opening at the hem. Turn coat and slip-stitch opening closed. Sew on fur trim and braid trim.

PINK DRESS

MATERIALS: Dress pattern in desired size. Fabric for dress according to pattern. White, pink fabric scraps. Organdy 10" × 12" for appliqué backing. Contrasting thread.

TO MAKE: Cut and assemble dress according to directions in pattern, but do not hem. Embroider front tucks in decorative machine stitches. Following directions on page 8, enlarge and trace appliqué pieces from Diagram 1. Cut appliqué pieces according to color and cutting key. Center a 10" × 12" piece of organdy on wrong side of dress front 1" above desired finished length with 12" edge parallel to bottom edge; baste. Baste appliqué pieces to dress in positions shown in Diagram 2. With contrasting thread, sew appliqués to dress with satin stitch covering raw edges. Add satin stitch to zig-zagged areas in Diagram 2. Cut away excess organdy close to satin stitch.

FURRY SLIPPER BOOTS

MATERIALS: Scraps of nonslippery fabric or soft leather or vinyl for soles. Scraps of fake fur for boots. Scraps of bias tape and decorative ribbon for trim.
TO MAKE: Make sole pattern by tracing outline of child's foot; add ½" all around for seam allowance. Measure sole from heel to toe at longest part, and enlarge Diagram 3 following directions on page 8 so bottom of boot is same measurement. Cut two boots on fold of fabric; cut two soles from nonslippery fabric or soft leather or vinyl. Right sides together, taking ½" seams, stitch toe. Center heel of sole at fold of boot. Stitch. Turn right-side out. Center a 24" tie on fold of boot (see Diagram), and tack at fold. Sew bias tape over raw edges, and add a decorative ribbon (see Diagram and photo).

CARROT T-SHIRT

MATERIALS: Purchased T-shirt in desired size. Scraps of orange fabric, green fabric and muslin for backing. Dark orange and green thread.
TO MAKE: Baste a piece of muslin to wrong side of shirt front; slightly stretching shirt. Enlarge Diagram 4 following directions on page 8. Use enlargement for pattern. Cut carrot appliqué from orange fabric and top from green fabric; baste to shirt and muslin close to raw edges. Sew over raw edges of appliqué and basting in satin stitch; add zig-zag stitching to carrot as indicated in Diagram 1. Trim away excess muslin close to stitching. Add zig-zag stitching over shoulder and armhole seams.

DIAGRAM 4

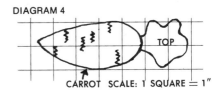

TOP

CARROT SCALE: 1 SQUARE = 1"

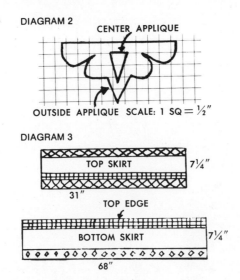

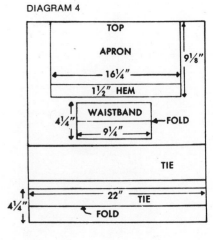

DIAGRAM 1

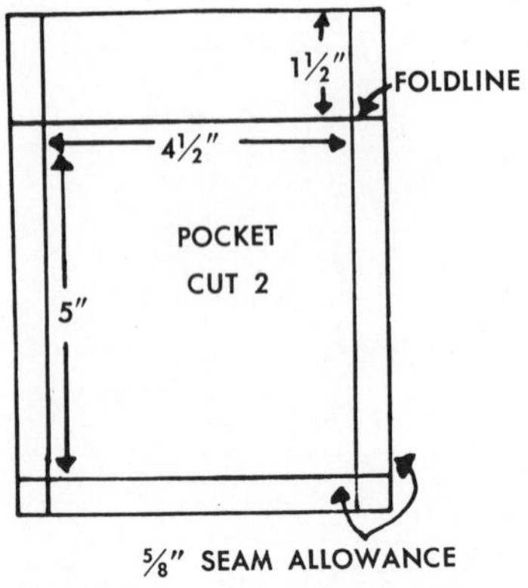

1½"

FOLDLINE

4½"

POCKET
CUT 2

5"

⅝" SEAM ALLOWANCE

DIAGRAM 2

CENTER APPLIQUE

OUTSIDE APPLIQUE   SCALE: 1 SQ = ½"

DIAGRAM 3

TOP SKIRT   7¼"

31"

TOP EDGE

BOTTOM SKIRT   7¼"

68"

DIAGRAM 4

TOP
APRON   9⅛"
16¼"
1½" HEM

WAISTBAND
4¼"   FOLD
9¼"

TIE

4¼"   22"   TIE

FOLD

PINAFORE AND DRESS

MATERIALS: Pinafore and dress patterns in desired size. Eyelet fabric for dress, solid and print fabrics for pinafore according to pattern. Pre-gathered lace for neck, cuffs and hem of dress. Rick-rack for pinafore yoke. Red scraps for hearts. 4 buttons. Embroidered ribbon for pinafore shoulder seams. Red and green thread.

TO MAKE: Cut and assemble dress according to pattern directions. Sew pre-gathered lace to neck, cuffs and hem. Cut and assemble pinafore according to pattern directions, remembering to add rick-rack below pinafore yoke. Make a paper pattern of a heart and cut two from red fabric. Baste to yoke front (see photo). Sew appliqué on with satin stitch, using green thread. Add decorative machine stitches around neck and armhole. Cover shoulder seam of pinafore with embroidered ribbon.

GREY TYROLEAN-STYLE JUMPER

MATERIALS: Pattern in desired size. Fabric according to pattern. 2" wide purchased embroidered trim. Fabric scrap for appliqué.

TO MAKE: Cut pattern according to layout. Cut two pockets according to size and shape in Diagram 1. Top stitch purchased embroidered trim to top of front (see photo). Sew jumper according to directions. Make pockets. Top stitch purchased embroidered trim to top of pocket. Center pockets on both sides of front. Baste and top stitch. Enlarge and trace appliqué pieces following directions on page 8. Using tracing as pattern, cut center appliqué from purchased embroidered trim. Cut outside appliqué from fabric scrap. Baste outside appliqué to center front of jumper, ¼" from bottom of embroidered trim at top. Place center appliqué on outside appliqué and baste. Using satin stitch to cover raw edges, sew center and outside appliqués to jumper. Make buttonholes on free ends of straps, and sew buttons to jumper back in desired positions.

PLAID PANTS

MATERIALS: Pants pattern in desired size. Fabric according to pattern. Ribbons of various widths.
TO MAKE: Cut and assemble pants according to pattern directions. Beginning at hem, slip-stitch ribbons over each leg (see photo).

NAVAJO SKIRT

Cut two pieces of fabric to sizes and shapes shown in Diagram 3, and add decorative trims as indicated. Gather top edge of bottom skirt and sew it to bottom edge of top skirt. Stitch a casing at waist and thread with elastic.

PATCHWORK DRESS AND APRON

MATERIALS: Dress pattern in desired size. Fabric according to pattern. (You can make patchwork fabric by sewing 2½" squares together until you have the desired amount of yardage.) Pre-gathered lace for neck and apron hem. Checked fabric, 22" × 24".
TO MAKE: For dress, cut and assemble according to pattern directions. Sew lace to neckline. For apron, cut 22" × 24" piece of checked fabric to size and shape in Diagram 4; ⅝" seam allowance is included. Turn ⅝" along apron sides to wrong side and stitch in place. Gather top edge of apron to 8". Stitch waistband to ties matching short ends; with right sides together fold waistband in half. Leaving 8" opening at waistband sew all other raw edges. Turn right side out. Press. Insert top of apron ⅝" into 8" opening in waistband; slip-stitch waistband to apron. Hem apron. Slip-stitch 15" piece of 2"-wide lace to right side of apron hem.

SHELL BACK

LEFT LEG

BOTTOM OF PANTS LEG

A   B   C   D   B   A

RIGHT ARM FLIP FOR LEFT ARM

RIGHT LEG

D

C

FROG PANTS

8"
4½"   BACK SEAM
       FRONT SEAM   9"
4½" ½"   ½"

LILY PADS, FROG, SNAILS AND WALRUS

MATERIALS: Naugahyde, 54″ wide: green for frog and lily pads—2 yds; brown for walrus—2⅔ yds; tan for snails–½ yd per snail; yellow, blue and pink–½ yd each; blue scraps for Walrus's bubbles. Fabric scraps, 10″ × 12″ lightweight: pink acetate jersey for pink lily; interesting floral motifs for snail; two 9″ squares of stripe jersey for frog's pants; white & yellow scraps for frog's eyes; unbleached muslin for walrus's tusks. Ballpoint needle size. Polyester Thread. Polyester fiberfill: 6 bags for walrus; 1 bag for frog and 2 lily-pads; 1½ bags for each snail. Brown paper for pattern.

TO MAKE: Because the edges do not fray, you can place pieces wrong sides together, and stitch close to the cut (or raw) edge. This saves turning the items and makes it easy to handle. **Cutting and stitching note:** Our designer has developed an easy method for sewing Naugahyde. Cut each back piece ¼″ larger than each front piece. Mark the finished edge with pen on the wrong side of the back piece. When stitching, match the front edge to the line on the back. This pen line makes it easy to match edges precisely while stitching. Otherwise, you might not notice if the back edge slips while stitching.

After stitching, simply trim the back edge even with front. **General how-to's:** Make paper pattern using brown paper. Cut out fronts first. Place each front over each back, wrong sides together, and trace outline to wrong side of back with pen. (This ensures that you will not cut out 2 fronts and ruin your Naugahyde.) Cut an extra ¼″ allowance around each back piece (see note above) Apply appliqué pieces to larger parts—such as eyes to frog, tusks and bubbles to walrus, and flowers to snail and lily pad. Stitch in the following order using an 8–10″ stitch length and a ¼″ seam allowance: mouth darts,
continued on page 110

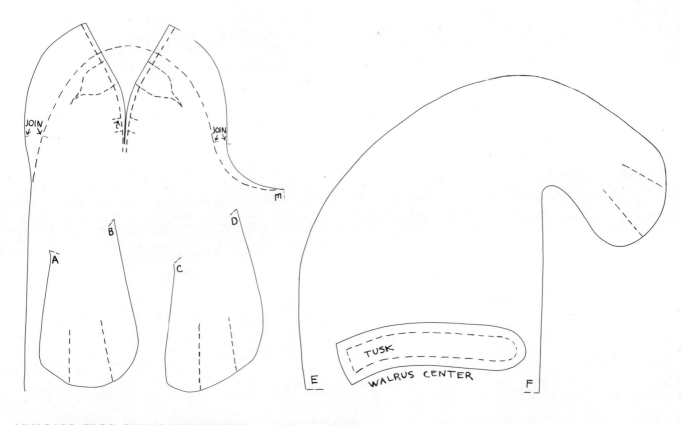

LILY PADS, FROG, SNAILS AND WALRUS continued from page 107

nose on walrus, eye darts, center front face seam. Stitch outside edge using the edge of presser foot as a guide and by matching front raw edge to pen line on back as described above. Leave a 5"–8" opening for stuffing. In some cases it may be easier to stuff as you go along. See special notes below. **Lily pads:** Apply pink lily with zigzag stitching. Stuff flower slightly and then stitch petal sections as indicated. Sew radial lines. Begin stitching inner curve, when you approach radial lines . . . stop with the needle in Naugahyde and stuff each section separately. Use a ruler to distribute stuffing evenly. **Frog:** Appliqué eyes to face using a zigzag stitch. Sew webbed toes & feet lines.

Stuff lower portion of arms and legs; stitch joints as indicated on pattern. Pants: Sew front and back seams half way down with a ½" seam. Then stitch inner leg seams. Turn and stitch ½" under at top and lower edges. Tack to frog body at sides. **Snails:** Stitch shell front from center outwards with a ¼" seam.

(NOTE: Front shell pattern includes extra allowance for variations that may occur in seaming. Before stitching front shell to snail, place on shell **back** pattern and trim off excess at bottom corner.) Blue/pink shell: Use same pattern as for yellow shell. Cut shell in half the entire length of swirl. Add ½" extra allowance to blue section which will lap over

pink. Then sew the shell the same way as above. Lap each shell section individually over front and back section body pieces, overlapping about ½". **Walrus:** Cut bubbles using a variety of cups and glasses. Stitch to front body. Tusks: Cut out shape from scrap Naugahyde along dotted line. Cut along solid line in muslin. Turn under edges of muslin around the shaped Naugahyde (this will give it body). Topstitch onto Walrus's body. Moustache: The wrong side of the Naugahyde is used for this. Cut 4 scrap pieces 3½" × 5". Cut ⅛" slits to within ½" from top. Stitch these to mouth after stitching dart. Stitch web lines on feet before stitching outer edge.

GINGHAM QUILT AND PILLOW

MATERIALS: Scraps of gingham fabric in assorted colors and check sizes. 1¾ yds of 45"-wide yellow and white gingham for backs of quilt and pillow. 15" × 20" piece of muslin or cheesecloth. Polyester fiberfill. 1½ yds of 2½"-wide pre-gathered eyelet ruffle. Scraps of 4-ply acrylic yarn for tufting. **NOTE:** Our quilt contains 56 gingham squares. It measures seven squares wide by eight long; quilt size can be enlarged by adding squares. Each finished square is 5–¾". The matching pillow is a rectangle composed of six squares.

TO MAKE: Quilt: From assorted gingham scraps, cut 56 squares, each 6¾" × 6¾". Taking ½" seams, stitch all squares together to form top of quilt. Cut yellow and white gingham for back of quilt to same size as top. Cut one thickness polyester fiberfill 2" larger than top all around. Place quilt top and back together, right sides out, with layer of polyester fiberfill between. Fasten all three layers together with long, hand-basting stitches, easing in padding. Begin in center and sew toward edge until there are a num-

ber of diagonal lines. Baste together around outside, about 2½" from raw edges. Leaving an unstitched border of one square all around, stitch by machine (about eight stitches per inch) through all layers to outline squares (Diagram 1). If necessary, trim away excess fiberfill. Turn 1" all around raw edges of top and backing to wrong sides; pin. Top-stitch two folded edges together close to outside edge (Diagram 2). Remove basting. Trim with tufts of yarn. To make each tuft, cut ten 1¼"-long pieces of yarn, and using more yarn, wrap bundle in center and stitch in place at points where patches meet (see photo). **Pillow:** From assorted ginghams, cut six squares, each 6¾" × 6¾". Taking ½" seams, stitch squares together to form pillow top measuring three squares by two squares. For back of pillow, cut yellow and white gingham to same size as top. Cut a piece of muslin or cheesecloth to same size as pillow top. Cut one thickness polyester fiberfill 2" larger than top all around. Baste one thickness of fiberfill between pillow top and muslin piece, as for quilt. To quilt pillow, machine stitch outlines of squares through all three layers. Trim away excess fiberfill if necessary. Pin gathered edge of eyelet ruffle to right side of quilted pillow top, around raw edges. Stitch ruffle in place. Place pillow back on quilted pillow top, right sides together, and stitch around three sides ½" from raw edges. (Be careful not to catch ruffle in seam.) Turn right-side out, stuff to desired plumpness, and slip-stitch opening closed. If desired, trim with tufts of yarn as for quilt.

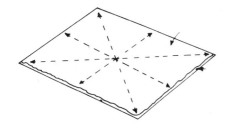

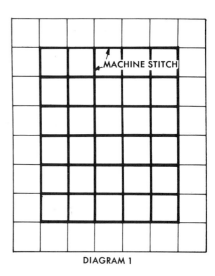

DIAGRAM 1

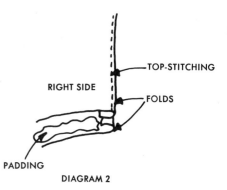

TOP-STITCHING

RIGHT SIDE

FOLDS

PADDING

DIAGRAM 2

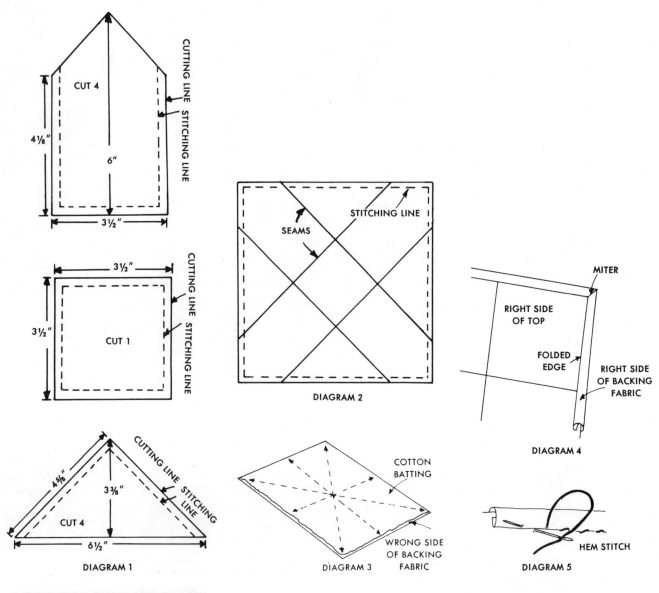

CUT 4

4⅛″

6″

3½″

CUTTING LINE
STITCHING LINE

3½″

3½″

CUT 1

CUTTING LINE
STITCHING LINE

CUTTING LINE

4⅝″

3⅜″

STITCHING LINE

CUT 4

6½″

DIAGRAM 1

STITCHING LINE

SEAMS

DIAGRAM 2

COTTON
BATTING

WRONG SIDE
OF BACKING
FABRIC

DIAGRAM 3

MITER

RIGHT SIDE
OF TOP

FOLDED
EDGE

RIGHT SIDE
OF BACKING
FABRIC

DIAGRAM 4

HEM STITCH

DIAGRAM 5

PATCHWORK QUILT AND PILLOW

MATERIALS: Cotton fabric scraps for patches—assorted small prints, stripes and plaids for triangles and oblongs, unbleached muslin for center squares. 2 yds of 45″ wide flower-sprigged cotton fabric for back of quilt. Cotton batting. Buttonhole twist. Scraps of yarn. Sharp needle, size 8–9. Cardboard. **NOTE:** Our quilt measures four patchwork blocks wide by five long. Each finished block is 9½″ square. The matching pillow is a rectangle composed of two patchwork blocks.

TO MAKE: Following Diagram 1, enlarge and make a cardboard pattern for each piece (¼″ seam allowance is included). Trace around pattern onto fabric. **For each patchwork block:** Cut one square from muslin; cut four triangles and four oblongs from assorted prints, stripes and plaids. If desired, write a family name and birthdate in center of each muslin square, using indelible ink. When stitching patches together, take ¼″ seams. Stitch two triangles to one oblong, matching 4⅝″ sides of triangles to 4⅛″

sides of oblong. Repeat. Stitch remaining two oblongs to two opposite sides of square, matching 3½″ edges. Press seams flat. Stitch the three 3-part sections together to form a 10″ block as shown in Diagram 2. Complete twenty blocks for quilt (or more if larger size is desired) and two for pillow. Taking ¼″ seams, join blocks to form quilt, according to dimensions given above. Press. Cut flower-sprigged fabric for back of quilt 2″ larger than top all around. Cut cotton batting to same size as backing. Place cotton batting on wrong side of backing, and fasten two layers together with long, hand-basting stitches. Begin in center and sew toward outer edge until there are a number of diagonal lines as shown in Diagram 3. Center top of quilt over other two layers; baste together diagonally as before. In addition, baste three layers together around outside edges. Starting at center, stitch by machine through all layers to **outline blocks.** Remove basting and trim away batting flush with edge of top. Trim edge of backing fabric to 1″ beyond top all around; turn ¼″ to wrong side along raw

edge and then turn this folded edge of backing ¼″ over edge of quilt top to form binding. Miter corners (Diagram 4). Pin, and then hemstitch folded edge in place by hand (Diagram 5). Use buttonhole twist to **outline individual patches** composing each block, stitching by hand through all layers close to seamlines of patches. For this hand stitching, use a very fine running stitch. Do a practice piece first and hold needle at right angles to quilt, pushing it straight up and down, rather than diagonally as in ordinary sewing. Push needle down and bring it back up near the point of entry. Tack small bows of yarn over top of quilt as desired. Join two remaining blocks for pillow top. Cut a piece of muslin to size of top, and a layer of batting 2″ larger all around. First make a padded top from these three layers, following quilt instructions above. Then cut print fabric for back 2″ larger all around. Join to padded top as for quilt, leaving one side open. Stuff with batting to desired plumpness, and slip-stitch to close opening. Decorate with yarn bows as desired.

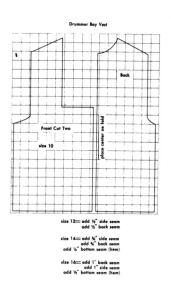

Drummer Boy Vest

Back

Front Cut Two

size 10

place center on fold

size 12== add ½" side seam
        add ½" back seam

size 14== add ¾" side seam
        add ¾" back seam
        add ¼" bottom seam (hem)

size 16== add 1" back seam
        add 1" side seam
        add ½" bottom seam (hem)

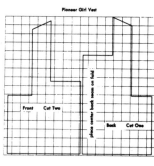

Pioneer Girl Vest

Front   Cut Two

place center back seam on fold

Back   Cut One

SCALE: 1 SQUARE = 1"

DRUMMER BOY VEST

NOTE: Read all instructions before proceeding.

MATERIALS: Pattern for vest (given). 26 yds of striped ribbon (you can substitute 1 yd of striped fabric). 1 yd of iron-on interfacing (woven). 1 yd red lining fabric. 8 gold eagle buttons. 1½ yds of gold narrow lacing.

TO MAKE: NOTE: Refer to photo if necessary. **Cut:** Cut the pattern from the interfacing, being sure to reverse second front piece to insure iron-on surface is on proper side. Pin ribbons in place, cutting the ribbon to proper length as you pin. Starting at center front, repeat pattern to side seam. Remove pins and iron in position, repeat procedure for vest back. **Sew:** With matching thread, top stitch ribbons to interfacing, leaving last row of side seam open; cut 1" wide strip of interfacing and apply to inside side seam. Press into place. Top stitch last side row of ribbon joining fronts and back. With shoulder seams open, trace vest outline on lining fabric; cut lining. Leaving shoulders and one center front seam open, sew lining to vest. Clip corners, turn right side out and press. To finish, machine stitch shoulder seams, slip stitch shoulder lining and center front. Cut two 18" long strips of ribbon, stitch ends, fold in half and press (epaulets made). Center on shoulder seams, stitch in place. Sew buttons in proper positions, lace the front with gold cord and tie.

PIONEER GIRL VEST

NOTE: Read all instructions before proceeding.

MATERIALS: Pattern for vest (given). ½ yd of polyester batting. ½ yd of red lining. 26 yds of striped ribbon (you can substitute 1 yd of striped fabric).

TO MAKE: NOTE: Refer to photo if necessary. **Cut:** Cut the pattern from the poly batting, pin ribbons in place. Start at center front, repeat pattern to side seam. **Sew:** With matching thread, top stitch ribbons to batting and leave last row of side seam open. Put batting side edges together, zig zag in place. Top stitch last row of ribbon back to front (covering batting side seam) and joining fronts and back. With shoulder seams open, trace vest on lining fabric; cut out. Stay stitch entire edge to lining; leaving 1" open at shoulder. Slip stitch edges at center front, turning lining under ¼", press. Bind armholes, neck and bottom edge with D. Stitch one edge of D to lining, fold over and top-stitch on the right side (fold corners at 90°). Stitch shoulder seams together; slip stitch shoulder lining seams. Cut six 1 yard strips of B (front ties). Stitch in proper position at front. Fasten with 3 bows at center front.

STOCKING DOLLS

MATERIALS: 2 large pairs of wool athletic socks. Buttons for features and garment trim. Scraps of denim. Edgings. Ribbon. Red bandana. Yarn for hair. Cotton batting. String.

TO MAKE: Stuff toe of one sock, forming a ball for head about 4½″ high. Tie with string for neck. Stuff body area about 8″ down from neck (this should take you partly into the ribbing of the sock). Stitch across. To make legs, cut up center of remaining ribbed cuff to the stitch line just made. Stitch up the inseam of each leg, stuff, stitch closed and tie string tightly for ankle, crotch to foot about 6¼″. To make arms use the ribbed portion of the second sock. Cut it in half lengthwise; stitch sides and top; stuff; close at other end and tie string tightly at wrist. Arms will be about 7½″ long. Attach arms to body. Stitch colored yarn to head in style

desired and use buttons for features. **Bandana shirt and dress:** (Both are made in the same way.) Fold bandana in half right sides facing. Make T-shape garment by cutting away a 5½″ square from each lower corner. (Bandana border should be at top of T.) Stitch under arm, shoulder and side seams. Make a casing at cuff and neck edge for ribbon or yarn drawstring. Hem bottom. Trim dress hem with lace or ribbon if desired. **Bandana scarf:** Make a 10″ square from bandana scraps. **Petticoat:** Gather strip of white cotton 5″ × 24″. Add decorative edging. **Apron:** Blue calico square 6″ × 6″, hem on 3 sides. Add decorative ribbon sash to gathering on 4th side. Add ribbon trim all around. **Overalls:** Enlarge overalls pattern as per instructions on page 8. Cut front in one piece, and one piece for back. Cut one pocket piece. Before stitching front and back

together apply decorative orange machine stitching to pocket; turn under hem on bib and suspenders; apply decorative stitching there as well. Apply pocket. Stitch sides and inseams. Press. Hem cuffs with orange decorative stitching. Tuck handkerchief in pocket and apply button trim if desired.

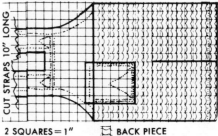

2 SQUARES = 1″   BACK PIECE

CARD TABLE PLAYHOUSE

MATERIALS: Card table (ours was 29″ square and 29″ high). Denim in required amount (our table required 4⅝ yds of 45″ wide fabric). Fabric and trimming scraps for appliqués. Fusible webbing.

TO MAKE: Measure around all four sides of top of card table and add 12″ to obtain measurement for skirt of cloth; cut fabric to this size. Turn 6″ at each end of skirt to wrong side so folded edges meet halfway between two table legs and form flap entrance. Mark hemline. Cut top to size, including seam allowance. Back fabric for appliqués with fusible webbing, following manufacturer's directions and cut out houses, rainbow, stars, clouds, etc. Appliqué houses and other cutouts to skirt and top of cloth in the most imaginative ways possible, maybe including your own house. With right sides facing and opening in skirt centered along one side of top, pin top to skirt. Stitch, hem bottom edge.

DIAGRAM 1

DIAGRAM 2

DOWNEAST GREG AND CONTENTED JENNY

SIZES: Jenny: 13½" high × 6½" wide;
Greg: 13½" high × 9½" wide.

MATERIALS: Jenny: ⅓ yd red knit, felt or sailcloth. Scraps of dark brown knit, fake fur or velour for bear. Unbleached muslin for face and hands. Green knit or contrasting color for collar and buttons. White knit for bow. Felt for eyes. Contrasting sewing thread for satin stitch. Red and black embroidery floss. Polyester stuffing. Heavy brown paper. Artist's tracing paper. **Greg:** ⅓ yellow knit, felt or sailcloth. Scraps of fake fur for beard. Red knit for lobster and pipe. Unbleached muslin for face and hands. Black or brown knit for boots. Black felt for buttons. Blue felt for eyes. 1" square of white fabric for "bandage". Contrasting sewing thread for satin stitch. Red and black embroidery floss. Polyester stuffing. Heavy brown paper. Artist's tracing paper.

TO MAKE: General Directions: Enlarge patterns in Diagrams 1 and 2. Cut out dolls from heavy brown paper and draw in details on both backs and fronts. To make patterns,

trace all details onto artist's tracing paper, following dotted lines where necessary when forms overlap. Leave ½" seam allowance around main body piece and hair for Jenny when cutting out. Do same for Greg, but trace boots separately from main body piece, leaving ½" seam allowance around them, too. Mark where boots should be placed on body by little snips into the seam allowance on either side. Do not leave seam allowances around any other pieces. **Jenny:** Follow General Directions. Cut out all pieces. Place face, hair and collar on front main body piece. Pin and hand baste in place. Using satin stitch on your sewing machine and contrasting thread (light thread on dark fabrics; dark thread on light fabrics), appliqué in place all at once. Place arm, hands and bear in position and appliqué in same manner. Place buttons and bear's nose in position and appliqué in place. Using buttonhole stitch, appliqué Jenny's eyes in place by hand, and embroider details in Jenny's and bear's face by hand. Place hair, buttons and bow in position on back main body piece; pin, baste and appliqué in same

manner as before. Be sure to outline knot in bow. With right sides together, sew front to back; make sure hair meets at sides. Leave an opening at bottom for turning. Clip and notch curves where necessary. Turn rightside out, stuff with polyester filling and slipstitch opening closed by hand. **Greg:** Follow General Directions. Cut out all pieces. Sew boots to proper areas on front and back main body pieces with straight stitching. Place face and beard on front main body piece. Pin, hand baste and appliqué in place using satin stitch on your sewing machine and contrasting thread (light thread on dark fabrics; dark thread on light fabrics). Stitch outline of brim and vertical line in hat with satin stitch. Stitch line down center of coat. Pin and baste lobster, hand, arm, pipe and buttons in place on front; stitch in place as before. Using buttonhole stitch, appliqué eyes by hand. Embroider nose and mouth by hand. On back, stitch outline of hat. Place arm, hand and bandage in position. Pin, baste and appliqué as before. Finish in same manner as Jenny, leaving opening for turning on side.

SMOCKED SUNDRESSES

SIZES: Children's 4–6X; girls' 8–12.
MATERIALS: 45" wide fabric for long or short children's dress; 54" wide fabric for long or short girls' dress. Long dress requires 1¾ yds. of fabric short dress requires 1¼ yds. 1¾ yds. 1" wide gros grain ribbon for long dress. 12" zipper. Bias binding or rick-rack to accommodate top width of fabric.
TO MAKE: Instructions are for all dresses. Use a 1 yd. length of fabric for long dress and 21" length for the short. This will allow for a deep, alterable hem. Cut fabric into a perfect rectangle making sure that edges are straight on all sides. Stitch bias binding (or rick-rack) along the top width of fabric in order to clean finish neckline. Measure down 1½" from neckline and begin stitching with elasticized thread parallel to the neckline across the width. Continue this procedure for 14 more rows, spacing each row ¼" apart. Fold fabric with right sides together lengthwise and baste stitch 1" away from selvedge for 12" along the length. Complete this seam using regular machine stitch. Press seam open. Using zipper foot, pin and stitch in a 12" zipper. Align top of zipper with first row of elasticized stitching. Cut four 14" strips of gros grain ribbon for long dress. For short dress, cut four strips of fabric 14" × 4", taking a ¼" seam lengthwise. Try dress on, keeping zipper at center back. Pin strips in place (see photo) along front and back neckline. Stitch on strips by hand with tack stitches below the first row of elasticized stitching. Put dress on child again. Tie strips into bows. Adjust dress on child. Pin hem length. Stitch seam binding onto raw hem edge, and stitch hem.

SUNBONNETS

Twenty" circle for hat: first make a 24" square from the fabric. Mark center and use a pin through the zero marking on your tape measure and the mark on the fabric as a marking around a 20" circle. (10" radius.) Stitch bias binding or rick-rack along the outside perimeter of the circle. On wrong side of fabric, stitch bias tape casing. (Fold ends under ½".) Leave opening at point where you begin casing for insertion of 26" length of ¼" elastic. Pull elastic through casing, stitch ends.

SIZE: 22½″ tall.

MATERIALS: Cotton broadcloth: light ochre, ⅔ yds; dark ochre, 18″ × 24″. Scraps of green, purple, hot pink, red, orange and yellow. Straight pins, scissors. Needle. Thread in dark ochre or in colors to match or contrast. Stuffing material (polyester, kapok or shredded foam). Dressmaker's carbon. Paper. Tracing wheel. Chalk marking pencil.

TO MAKE: Most of this doll is done by reverse appliqué, a technique used by the Cuna Indians of the San Blas Islands off Panama. The technique is used to create their "molas", (yoked, short-sleeved blouses). Modern stitchery enthusiasts have been adopting the technique for decorative wall art and, as any other needle art, it can be used for wearing apparel, accessories and interior decor. The only conventional appliqué is done on the cheeks and the outer edge. Following our enlarging technique on page 8, trace the doll pattern onto the dark ochre (do not cut away). On shapes that have smaller shapes within, trace only the outer shapes. For face omit all but outer circle. Use color of carbon with least contrast. Follow photograph for color guide. Start first with the face outer circle. Cut "hole" leaving at least ¼″ inside the circle for turning under. Clip this edge about every ⅜″ close but not touching the traced edge. Cut a circle from green about 1″ larger than the traced circle. Pin it to the ochre underneath making sure it covers the "hole" Whip down the ochre edge to the green by folding under on the traced line, using very tiny stitches about 3/16″ apart. (See Figure 1.) When it is sewn, turn the work over and trim the excess edge from green. For the next inner circle, (pink) trace or draw freehand the circle pattern onto the green and repeat process using hot pink. Repeat again using the previously cut away green circle. Repeat again using the yellow. **Begin face details:** trace eyebrow, outer eye, nose and lip shapes. Omit cheeks. Repeat same technique described above. As inner shapes get smaller, instead of tracing from pattern, it is easier to draw them in freehand lightly with a chalk pencil. **Hints for nose and other angular shapes:** Clip inward corners to turn edges under. On outward corners, trim excess fabric away. Corners can be a bit stubborn. A drop of water will make them easier to handle. Use needle as a tool to force them under. Always place a stitch right at the corner. Sometimes a dot of white glue worked into place with your needle can be used to keep them down. A few frayed corners here and there are not objectionable. For small and narrow shapes, fabric is only slit instead of cut away. Always allow as much as possible for turning under. (See Figure 2.) Continue with rest of doll. On complicated shapes like the coils on the chest, slit only a little at a time, whip down and slit further. For cheeks, trace circle and inner shapes onto orange. Slit inner shapes and appliqué to pink. Cut orange leaving at least ¼″ around. Clip and pin into position on face and hem down, using conventional appliqué. (See Figure 3.) **Final assembly:**

When entire design is complete, trim dark ochre leaving ⅜″ all around. Cut light ochre fabric in half so you have two pieces 18″ × 24″. On one piece, pin doll and conventional appliqué the edge, clipping and trimming corners as you work. Then with chalk pencil place marks on the edge ½″ from dark ochre edge. Place tracing paper underneath with carbon side touching wrong side of doll. With tracing wheel connect markings. Curve at inward points and around hands instead of drawing angles. Remove the carbon paper and you will have the doll outline on the reverse side. Place doll face down to the second piece of light ochre and pin together. On sewing machine or by hand, stitch on traced line leaving one side of doll unseamed. Trim around leaving ½″ seam. Clip corners and curves and turn right side out. Insert stuffing, starting with points on head, then head, feet, legs, hands, arms and body. Close side with blind stitch, stuffing as you sew.

FIGURE 1

FIGURE 2

Sun doll shown on page 72; instructions, page 121.

FIGURE 3

EDGE OF UNDER FABRIC

TRACED EDGE

CLIPPED EDGE

HALF-PATTERN FOR SUN DOLL

¼ ACTUAL SIZE

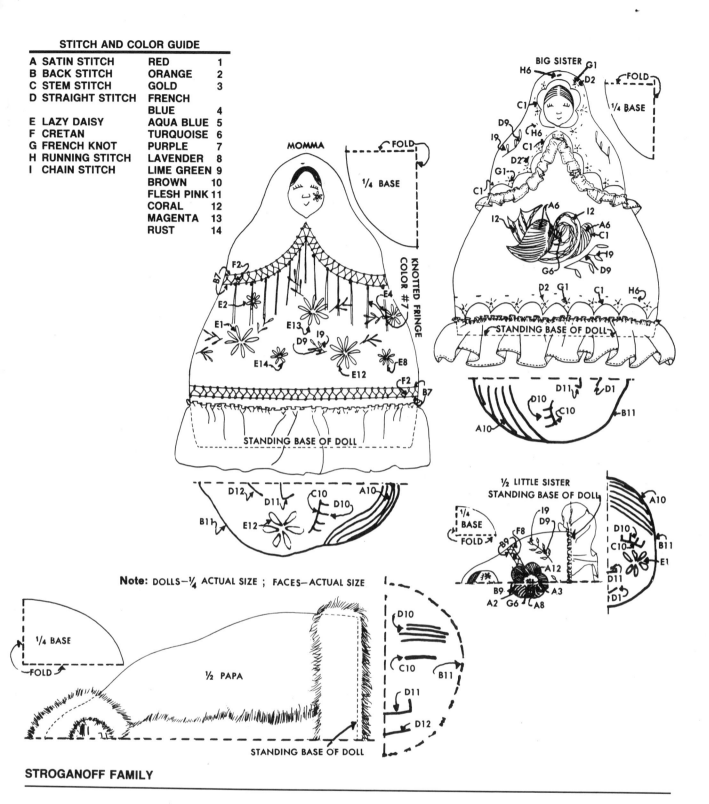

STITCH AND COLOR GUIDE

A	SATIN STITCH	RED	1
B	BACK STITCH	ORANGE	2
C	STEM STITCH	GOLD	3
D	STRAIGHT STITCH	FRENCH BLUE	4
E	LAZY DAISY	AQUA BLUE	5
F	CRETAN	TURQUOISE	6
G	FRENCH KNOT	PURPLE	7
H	RUNNING STITCH	LAVENDER	8
I	CHAIN STITCH	LIME GREEN	9
		BROWN	10
		FLESH PINK	11
		CORAL	12
		MAGENTA	13
		RUST	14

Note: DOLLS—¼ ACTUAL SIZE ; FACES—ACTUAL SIZE

STROGANOFF FAMILY

SIZES AND MATERIALS: Poppa: (13″ high without fur); ½ yd rust wool; 1⅓ yds of 1″ wide real or fake fur banding. **Momma:** (12″ high without ruffle); ½ yd black velveteen. **Big Sister:** (10¾″ high without ruffle); ½ yd purple cotton. **Little Sister:** (4¾″ high without ruffle); ¼ yd red cotton. Kapok or cotton batting for stuffing. Six-strand embroidery floss (colors listed below). Crewel needle. Unbleached muslin for faces. Embroidery hoop.

TO MAKE: Enlarge doll patterns according to instructions on page 8, leaving enough fabric around traced pattern to easily handle your embroidery. Embroider doll following stitch and color chart. Cut way excess fabric leaving ½″ seam allowance. For each doll, attach face (see below); sew front and back sides together; turn right side out; stuff (packing well); sew on base adding more stuffing as needed. Make and attach ruffles and fur banding as indicated. **Faces:** Trace face pattern onto a piece of muslin. Following stitch chart, embroider face. Cut out face leaving ½″ seam allowance. Using sewing thread, sewing running stitches around face outline and pull-up so face has slightly 'puffed' effect. Turn ½″ seam margin under; attach face using small blind stitches around ¾ of face; stuff face and then complete attachment.

NOTE—Embroidery for back: Little Sister: Motif same except Cretan banding dips slightly to form wide 'V' and floral motif drops just below 'V.' **Big Sister:** No embroidery in back but ruffle continues around. **Momma:** Both Cretan bandings continue to back, top one dipping slightly to form wide 'V.' Scatter similar flowers in back. **Poppa:** Fur continues at back hem and at back of head as a hat.

746.4
CRE   Creative Sewing

      By the editors of Ladies'
      Home Journal Needle & Craf

DATE DUE

1981	JUL 13 '93		
JAN 15 1982			
MAR 1 6 1982			
APR 1 2 1983			
AUG 11 1983			
MAR 1 1984			
FEB 2 0 1985			
APR 2 1986			
AUG 2 1988			
FEB 1 9 1991			